Managing IaaS and DBaaS Clouds with Oracle Enterprise Manager Cloud Control 12c

Implement comprehensive cloud computing solutions efficiently using Oracle Enterprise Manager

Ved Antani

BIRMINGHAM - MUMBAI

Managing IaaS and DBaaS Clouds with Oracle Enterprise Manager Cloud Control 12*c*

First published: November 2013

Production Reference: 1181113

Published by Packt Publishing Ltd.
Livery Place
35 Livery Street
Birmingham B3 2PB, UK.

ISBN 978-1-78217-770-8

www.packtpub.com

Cover Image by Abhishek Pandey (abhishek.pandey1210@gmail.com)

Credits

Author
Ved Antani

Reviewers
Stuart Murray
Kevin L. Jackson

Acquisition Editor
Owen Roberts

Commissioning Editor
Deepika Singh

Technical Editors
Hardik B. Soni
Dennis John
Pramod Kumavat

Project Coordinator
Michelle Quadros

Proofreader
Katherine Tarr

Indexer
Monica Ajmera Mehta

Graphics
Ronak Dhruv

Production Coordinator
Kirtee Shingan

Cover Work
Kirtee Shingan

About the Author

Ved Antani started programming on IBM PC-AT using QBasic and Pascal. He has 10000 hours of practice using several programming languages such as Java, Python, and Erlang. He spends quite a lot of time writing middleware and massively scalable game servers. When not trying to prove someone wrong on the Internet, Ved enjoys functional programming on Erlang or Elixir. Ved wishes he were a classical pianist and not a software engineer. He currently works as Technical Director with Electronic Arts.

I would like to thank my parents and my wife Meghna for their support and making sure I get constant supply of caffeine. I would also like to thank my two year old son, Utsav, for not destroying the laptop on which this text was written.

About the Reviewers

Stuart Murray has worked internationally in the IT industry for over 25 years, helping clients derive value from their investments. His experience re-architecting the IT service departments of client organizations has led to the alignment of IT with the business and has made the provision of services significantly more effective and efficient.

With experience leading engagements in business architecture, application architecture, data architecture, and technology architecture as well as process re-engineering, Stuart has created a datacenter product framework incorporating business and operational practices and a datacenter processing model to return superior efficiency and flexibility into major institutions.

He has extensive experience in application dependency analysis allowing highly optimized and risk averse datacenter migration strategies and plans to be developed.

A passion for delivering value through technology and the application of technology to deliver real business benefit are key drivers in Stuart's ideology.

He has written several articles for trade journals and has delivered talks on end-to-end service management and the journey to the cloud.

I would like to thank my wife Meredith for her support while reviewing the text of this book. Without her perseverance late at night, the reviews would simply have not happened.

Kevin L. Jackson is a senior information technologist specializing in information technology solutions that meet critical Federal Government operational requirements. Currently he serves as Vice President and General Manager, Cloud Services with NJVC, one of the largest IT solutions providers supporting the United States Department of Defense.

Before joining NJVC, Mr. Jackson served in various senior management positions with Dataline, LLC; Cryptek Inc.; IBM; and JP Morgan Chase. In 2012, he was named *Cyber Security Visionary* by *U.S. Black Engineer and Information Technology* magazine. Mr. Jackson retired from the U.S. Navy, earning specialties in Space Systems Engineering, Airborne Logistics, and Airborne Command and Control. He also served with the National Reconnaissance Office, Operational Support Office, providing tactical support to Navy and Marine Corps forces worldwide.

Mr. Jackson is the founder and author of Cloud Musings (`http://kevinljackson.blogspot.com`) and the Founder and Editor of Government Cloud Computing on Ulitzer electronic magazine (`http://govcloud.ulitzer.com`). His first book, *GovCloud: Cloud Computing for the Business of Government, Government Training Inc.*, was released in March 2011. Kevin is a co-author of the Intelligence and National Security Alliance whitepaper entitled *Cloud Computing: Risks, Benefits, and Mission Enhancement for the Intelligence Community.*

Kevin has been deeply involved in the broad collaborative effort between industry and the U.S. National Institute of Standards and Technology on the Federal Government's adoption of cloud computing technologies. He is the Chairman of the Network Centric Operations Industry Consortium's Cloud Computing Working Group, and his formal education includes a Master of Science, Electrical Engineering (Computer Engineering), a Master of Arts degree in National Security and Strategic Studies, and a Bachelor of Science degree in Aerospace Engineering.

www.PacktPub.com

Support files, eBooks, discount offers and more

You might want to visit www.PacktPub.com for support files and downloads related to your book.

Did you know that Packt offers eBook versions of every book published, with PDF and ePub files available? You can upgrade to the eBook version at www.PacktPub.com and as a print book customer, you are entitled to a discount on the eBook copy. Get in touch with us at service@packtpub.com for more details.

At www.PacktPub.com, you can also read a collection of free technical articles, sign up for a range of free newsletters and receive exclusive discounts and offers on Packt books and eBooks.

http://PacktLib.PacktPub.com

Do you need instant solutions to your IT questions? PacktLib is Packt's online digital book library. Here, you can access, read and search across Packt's entire library of books.

Why Subscribe?

- Fully searchable across every book published by Packt
- Copy and paste, print and bookmark content
- On demand and accessible via web browser

Free Access for Packt account holders

If you have an account with Packt at www.PacktPub.com, you can use this to access PacktLib today and view nine entirely free books. Simply use your login credentials for immediate access.

Instant Updates on New Packt Books

Get notified! Find out when new books are published by following @PacktEnterprise on Twitter, or the *Packt Enterprise* Facebook page.

Table of Contents

Preface

Cloud computing has become a ubiquitous buzzword in the software industry. While almost everyone was trying to define what cloud computing actually meant, few people realized that cloud computing is in fact an old idea. The term "cloud computing" is an attempt to group a lot of standard technologies under one umbrella and combine all of these little pieces into a unified shared infrastructure. Cloud computing essentially solves the problem of scale — a problem which otherwise seemed too daunting.

As we move towards massively scaled interconnected software systems, chances are that you will develop and deploy the software for the cloud. Cloud computing sounds like the solution to all the problems related to scalability and fault-tolerant software, but in reality, getting cloud infrastructure right is a very difficult task.

Luckily, over the years, technology that supports cloud computing has stabilized and standardized a lot. Many interesting solutions have been proposed and some wonderful tools have been field-tested in the industry. The most important innovation that really changed the way people used shared infrastructure has been Amazon's Elastic Cloud platform. EC2 demonstrated that cloud could serve massively scalable software systems with superb fault tolerance and performance guarantees.

Enterprise software vendors realized that they will have to embrace the cloud model to offer extremely cost-effective and easy-to-manage software delivery. This realization drove major software companies such as Oracle, VMware, Microsoft, and others to focus on making their enterprise software cloud ready.

Oracle Enterprise Manager offers a great environment for building cloud computing platforms for your enterprise. Oracle Enterprise Manager combines various technologies such as Oracle Database, clustering, virtualization, and network to offer a single solution. As we will see in this book, creating a self-service model of cloud provisioning is extremely streamlined with Oracle Enterprise Manager. Oracle Enterprise Manager supports most complex chargeback models and offers great flexibility in designing your own system of chargeback. We will take a detailed look at the various capabilities of Oracle Enterprise Manager and how we can effectively utilize them.

What this book covers

Chapter 1, Setting Up Enterprise Manager, covers important bits of information to correctly set up Enterprise Manager.

Chapter 2, Infrastructure as a Service, illustrates all the steps necessary to set up an IaaS using Enterprise Manager.

Chapter 3, Database as a Service, covers several DBaaS topologies and techniques in detail.

Chapter 4, Enterprise Monitoring, walks through the chargeback models offered by Enterprise Manager and how to optimize them.

Chapter 5, Cloud APIs, gives an overview of the usage of the programmable interface of Enterprise Manager using the various cloud REST APIs and CLIs.

What you need for this book

Depending on what you want to achieve, you will need a different set of software and hardware. The installation of Oracle Enterprise Manager comes bundled with most of the necessary software, but you should make sure you read the official documentation accompanying your installation media. You must have a working Java installation on the operating system you are planning to use to install Enterprise Manager.

Who this book is for

This book is written as a hands-on guide rather than a text on cloud computing. It is assumed that the reader has an understanding of the basic building blocks of cloud computing , such as networking, virtualization, and storage. This book will help you use and set up Oracle Enterprise Manager features. It is aimed at cloud administrators and users of self-service provisioning systems offered by Enterprise Manager. This book also helps administrators who want to understand the chargeback mechanism offered by Enterprise Manager.

Conventions

In this book, you will find a number of styles of text that distinguish between different kinds of information. Here are some examples of these styles, and an explanation of their meaning.

Code words in text are shown as follows: "All the resource models support JSON payloads and defined by media type `application/oracle.com.cloud.common.DbPlatformInstance+json`."

A block of code is set as follows:

```
<AGENT_HOME>/bin/emctl secure add_trust_cert_to_jks -trust_certs_loc
<location of the certificate> -alias
```

Any command-line input or output is written as follows:

```
$<DB_HOME>/assistants/dbca/templates
```

New terms and **important words** are shown in bold. Words that you see on the screen, in menus or dialog boxes for example, appear in the text like this: "Select **OMS Shared Filesystem** from the administration page."

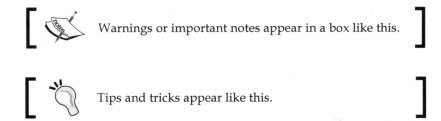

Warnings or important notes appear in a box like this.

Tips and tricks appear like this.

Reader feedback

Feedback from our readers is always welcome. Let us know what you think about this book—what you liked or may have disliked. Reader feedback is important for us to develop titles that you really get the most out of.

To send us general feedback, simply send an e-mail to feedback@packtpub.com, and mention the book title via the subject of your message.

If there is a topic that you have expertise in and you are interested in either writing or contributing to a book, see our author guide on www.packtpub.com/authors.

Customer support

Now that you are the proud owner of a Packt book, we have a number of things to help you to get the most from your purchase.

Errata

Although we have taken every care to ensure the accuracy of our content, mistakes do happen. If you find a mistake in one of our books—maybe a mistake in the text or the code—we would be grateful if you would report this to us. By doing so, you can save other readers from frustration and help us improve subsequent versions of this book. If you find any errata, please report them by visiting http://www.packtpub. com/submit-errata, selecting your book, clicking on the **errata submission form** link, and entering the details of your errata. Once your errata are verified, your submission will be accepted and the errata will be uploaded on our website, or added to any list of existing errata, under the Errata section of that title. Any existing errata can be viewed by selecting your title from http://www.packtpub.com/support.

Piracy

Piracy of copyright material on the Internet is an ongoing problem across all media. At Packt, we take the protection of our copyright and licenses very seriously. If you come across any illegal copies of our works, in any form, on the Internet, please provide us with the location address or website name immediately so that we can pursue a remedy.

Please contact us at copyright@packtpub.com with a link to the suspected pirated material.

We appreciate your help in protecting our authors, and our ability to bring you valuable content.

Questions

You can contact us at questions@packtpub.com if you are having a problem with any aspect of the book, and we will do our best to address it.

1
Setting Up Enterprise Manager

Cloud computing has changed the way enterprise software is developed and deployed. Cloud computing is becoming the obvious choice for large scale software deployments because of the various cost benefits it offers. Cloud platforms eliminate the need for setting up costly hardware to host your applications. Your applications are hosted on a shared platform managed by specialists. You can focus on building your application and not really involved in managing the platform. Though there are modern software that make it easier to deploy a scalable cloud infrastructure, there are no single-click solutions available yet. This book focuses on two varieties of cloud deployments: **IaaS (Infrastructure as a Service)** and **DBaaS (Database as a Service)**. We are going to explore **Oracle Enterprise Manager Cloud Control 12***c* to implement these two flavors of Cloud Computing. Oracle's Enterprise Manager is an interesting tool because it combines the prowess of Oracle's Database (though you can configure other databases), Fusion Middleware, as well as virtualization technologies. Oracle Enterprise Manager has quickly established itself as an end-to-end cloud management system. Organizations like CERN have utilized Enterprise Manager to extend their existing Oracle Grid databases and WebLogic Server infrastructure into a scalable elastic cloud.

This book will cover these specific scenarios and we will assume that the reader is familiar with the common components involved in building the cloud platform. We assume that the reader knows the basics of networking, storage, and has a working knowledge of command-line tools. This book takes a hands-on tutorial approach and targets specific areas to achieve the most productive setup of Oracle Enterprise Manager.

This chapter focuses on making sure the basic setup is complete before we start with the complex scenarios of implementing IaaS and DBaaS.

Topics covered in this chapter:

- Setting up Software Library
- Discovering and adding targets
- Creating a database instance for Enterprise Manager
- Executing Prerequisite Kit Utility

Setting up Software Library

Enterprise Manager is bundled with Software Library, a repository of a number of application software, VM images, and custom scripts used with Oracle Enterprise Manager. Software Library offers useful versioning and patching mechanisms to manage the software. We are going to cover the basic setup for Software Library.

Software Library can be accessed by navigating to **Enterprise | Provisioning and Patching | Software Library**.

Inside the Software Library page, you will find two types of software sources listed: **Oracle-owned folders** (tagged by a lock icon) and **User-owned folders**. Oracle-owned content is shipped with Enterprise Manager. On the other hand, user-owned folders, as the name suggests, are created by users to organize custom entities.

There are a few things that we need to configure before we can start using the Software Library. We will need to configure the storage repository and add an **Upload File Storage Location**. Make sure this location is on a host where OMS is already running. You can also configure a **Referenced File Location**, which is a read-only location.

Setting up the storage location

We will discuss ways to configure storage location for the software library. This location is used to upload software library entities and artifacts.

The OMS Agent Filesystem location

The Select the **OMS Agent Filesystem** option and click on **+Add**. You will need to provide the following details:

- **Name**: It is unique for the storage location (for example, shared_fs).

- **Host**: This is the location where OMS is running. You can either manually enter the value of the host or search inside the dialog box.

- **Location**: When you open the search dialog in the **Location** textbox, you will need to log in to the host machine. Once you are logged in, you can select the location where you want to create the agent filesystem.

This action triggers a metadata registration job which can be monitored for completion by refreshing the screen or clicking on **Show Detailed Results**.

The OMS Shared Filesystem location

You can also set up the storage location as an OMS shared filesystem location. This option sometimes comes in handy when you already have an OMS running.

1. Select **OMS Shared Filesystem** from the administration page.

2. Click on **+Add** and provide the name of the OMS's host where you want the upload location to be defined and specify the OMS's host address.

Referenced file location

You can configure a storage location that can be used for referring to files from the Software Library entities.

1. Select **Referenced File Location** on the **Library Administration** page.

2. You can either add an HTTP location or an NFS location as referenced file location:

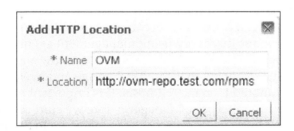

3. Enter a name for the referenced file location and an HTTP location path for the storage server that you want to be referenced in the **Add HTTP Location** dialog.

4. If you are adding an NFS location, select **NFS** from the storage type list and add the NFS server details. This value is typically an IP address or a fully qualified domain name for the NFS host (for example, `10.10.90.1` or `nfs_service_1.main_domain.domain`).

Discovering and adding targets

Components of IaaS or DBaaS such as Oracle Database instances or Oracle WebLogic servers are called targets. The Enterprise Manager lets you monitor these targets inside a unified console, making it very easy to have a real-time view of the entire cloud implementation. Before we can start monitoring the targets, we need to install management agents on those targets. Targets can be either added manually or discovered automatically through a few additional steps. We will briefly look at both of these processes without going into much of the implementation details.

Automatic discovery and promotion

In automatic discovery, a management agent usually runs on the host. This agent scans for unmanaged hosts. When an unmanaged host is found, they can be converted to managed hosts. On managed hosts, targets can be searched and promoted to managed targets. Setting up automatic discovery using management agents is an involved process and requires proper set up of NMap binaries to allow a network scan. The network scan can be restricted to a specific IP range and eventually these network scanned targets are promoted to managed hosts. It is important to ensure we have the added necessary targets to Enterprise Manager before we start configuring them. To discover unmanaged hosts using network scan, navigate to **Setup | Add Target | Configure Auto Discovery**. Click on the **Configure** button to configure network scan settings. You can create a new network scan configuration or edit an existing one.

You can provide IP address ranges (for example, `10.0.0-255.1-250`) in the scan table or provide specific hostnames. You can submit the scan once the settings are correctly configured. Once the hosts are discovered, you can go ahead and convert unmanaged hosts into managed hosts. For this, navigate to **Setup** | **Add Target** | **Auto Discovery Results**. You will find all discovered hosts under the **Network-scanned Targets** tab. From this table, select all the unmanaged hosts and click on the **Promote** button.

Adding targets manually

Unmanaged hosts can be converted into managed hosts by installing the **Management Agent** on each host. The **Add Host Wizard** is used to add targets using the guided process.

Creating a database instance for Enterprise Manager

We will need to configure the underlying Oracle database instance to hold the Enterprise Manager data and artifacts before we can do anything useful with Enterprise Manager. While the Enterprise Manager installer can configure the database for you, we recommend you do it beforehand to make sure there are no errors in this very critical step.

Oracle provides pre-configured and tested sets of database templates. You can download these templates from `http://www.oracle.com/technetwork/oem/enterprise-manager/downloads/db-templates-1959276.html`. Please do make sure that you are downloading the correct version of the database template for your Operation System. After downloading this template, extract the template into the following location on your Oracle database host:

`$<DB_HOME>/assistants/dbca/templates`

For example,

`D:\app\oracle\product\12.1.0\dbhome_1\assistants\dbca\templates`
(on Windows machines)

Create the database in Advanced mode by running Oracle Database Configuration Assistant from <DB_HOME>/bin/dbca. On the **Database Template** screen, select the template which is suitable for your deployment:

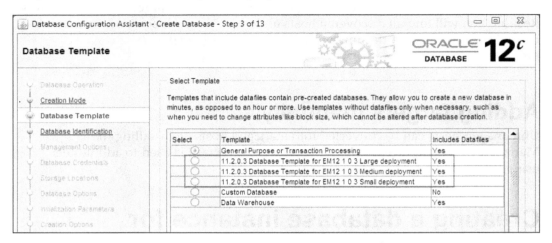

When you run Oracle Database Configuration Assistant, the option **Configure Enterprise Manager (EM) Database Express** is checked by default. Make sure you uncheck it:

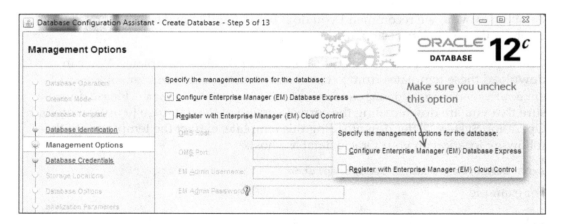

One final step to verify all the necessary setup is done, is to run the Prerequisite Kit script. The nice thing about this tool is that it detects incorrect configuration problems and tries to fix them, if possible. When you install Enterprise Manager, the installation wizard runs this script as a part of the installation process, but we can run this script standalone to make sure all configurations are correct.

Running Prerequisite Kit scripts from Software Kit

The Prerequisite Kit is available in the following location of the downloaded Enterprise Manager:

`<download location of the script>/install/requisites/bin/emprereqkit` (on Microsoft Windows, the namefilename is `emprereqkit.bat`)

Example: `D:\OracleMS\install\requisites\bin` (on Windows path)

To run this prerequisite script without taking any corrective actions, we can run it as follows:

`<download location>/install/requisites/bin/emprereqkit -executionType <install/upgrade/postrequisite/plugindeploy> -prerequisiteXMLLoc <prerequisite_xml_location> -connectString <connection_string> -dbUser SYS -dbPassword <password_for_sys_account> -dbRole sysdba -reposUser SYSMAN -showPrereqs`

For example on a Windows installation:

`D:\OracleMS\install\requisites\bin\emprereqkit.bat`

`-executionType install`

`-prerequisiteXMLLoc $ORACLE_HOME/install/requisites/list/`

`-connectString "(DESCRIPTION=(ADDRESS_LIST=(ADDRESS=(PROTOCOL=TCP) (HOST=localhost)(PORT=1521)))(CONNECT_DATA=(SID=EnterpriseManager)))"`

`-dbUser SYS`

`-dbPassword mypwd`

`-dbRole sysdba`

`-reposUser SYSMAN`

`-showPrereqs`

If you want to take corrective actions, you can use the flag `--runCorrectiveActions` in the script.

Summary

This was a whirlwind tour of **Oracle Enterprise Manager Cloud Control**. We could have only scratched the surface of all the setup required to get started, but that was the idea of this chapter. We have seen how to verify the most critical pieces of the setup so that we are equipped to move ahead and take a detailed look at more advanced use cases of building an Infrastructure as a Service, which will be the focus of our next chapter.

2
Infrastructure as a Service

Now that we have made sure that all the necessary pieces are in place, we can start implementing a basic **Infrastructure as a Service** model using the Oracle Enterprise Manager Cloud Control 12*c*.

The IaaS model is essentially an abstraction of shared resources such as hardware, storage, and networks. The key here is that these abstract pieces of virtualized resources are provisioned on-demand according to various service levels and can be billed on the basis of actual usage (for example, storage for 1 GB may be charged at $0.00020 an hour or $0.15 a month). IaaS allows businesses to rent these virtualized computing resources instead of buying and maintaining permanent hardware. Most IaaS services offer self-service portals to provision resources. IaaS providers also provide configurable chargebacks and reporting capabilities. Correct chargeback and monitoring helps maintain SLA transparency from the provider as well as the consumer side. Oracle Enterprise Manager offers robust capabilities to manage a scalable IaaS. In this chapter, we are going to take a detailed look at some of the important aspects of setting up IaaS on Oracle Enterprise Manager.

IaaS fits well into both public as well as private cloud implementations, and most of the topologies such as storage and virtualization remain the same between these two flavors. IaaS providers offer virtualized compute resources using **Virtual Machines (VM)** based on operating system templates (for example, Amazon AMI) and persistent storage that can be provisioned for various sizes. Virtualization coupled with the elasticity of resources make IaaS a great option.

We will assume that the reader has sufficient knowledge of the terminologies used in this chapter and a basic understanding of the navigation around EM.

The topics covered in this chapter are as follows:

- Oracle VM Manager setup and registration
- Networking

- Configuring storage servers
- Creating and configuring virtual server pools
- Monitoring and administering IaaS
- Setting up the IaaS self-service portal

The Oracle VM Manager setup and registration

As we discussed earlier, virtualization is the key to IaaS. Oracle VM Manager (part of Enterprise Manager) is a single interface that allows for the management of virtualized resources for your IaaS. VM Manager is the place where you create and manage virtual machines, guest VMs, virtual server pools, and zones for your IaaS. The first thing you need do is to register the VM Manager by adding it as an Enterprise Manager target (refer to the *Adding targets manually* section in *Chapter 1, Setting Up Enterprise Manager*).

Before you add Oracle VM Manager as an EM target, make sure you have imported VM Manager certificates in the agent keystore by performing the following:

1. Export the VM Manager certificate by executing the following command on your VM Manager host:

   ```
   <JAVA_HOME>/bin/keytool -keystore <VMMANAGER_HOME>/ovmmCoreTcps.ks
   -exportcert -alias ovmm -file <location of the certificate>
   ```

2. Import the VM Manager certificate by executing the command on the agent host:

   ```
   <AGENT_HOME>/bin/emctl secure add_trust_cert_to_jks -trust_certs_
   loc <location of the certificate> -alias <alias>
   ```

To add the VM Manager as an Enterprise Manager target, perform the following steps:

1. Navigate to the **Enterprise | Cloud | Infrastructure Home | Register OVM Manager**.

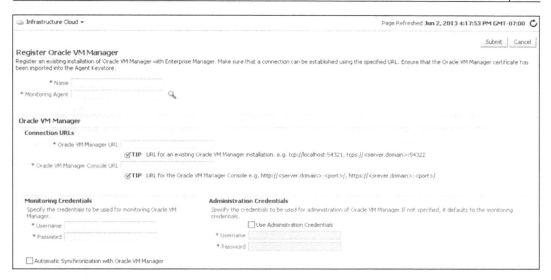

2. Enter values in the **Name** and **Monitoring Agent** fields.

3. Under **Connection URLs**, make sure you adhere to the format displayed in the tooltips. For the VM Manager URL, the format is of the type:

   ```
   tcp://localhost:<port> or tcps://<hostname:<port>
   ```

   For the VM Manager Console URL, the format is of the type:

   ```
   https://<hostname>:<port>
   ```

4. Enterprise Manager can automatically monitor virtualization targets and VM Manager. If you select the **Automatic Synchronization** checkbox, all changes on the VM Manager are reflected on Enterprise Manager automatically at a regular interval (defaults to 1 min). If you don't want to automatically sync the changes to EM, you can manually synchronize by right-clicking on the VM Manager target and selecting **Synchronize**.

Discovering Oracle VM Manager

We discussed how we can manually register Oracle VM Managers to be managed by Oracle Enterprise Manager. If we want to automatically scan and detect unknown OVM Hosts, we can use the Automatic Discovery feature.

1. Navigate to **Enterprise Manager | Setup | Add Target | Configure Auto Discovery** (log in as super admin).

2. Click on the **Configure Network Scan Discovery** icon and in the **Network Scan Discovery** page, click on **Create**.

3. In the next screen, you can configure the network scan discovery options. You can create new network discovery scan options as well as edit the existing ones.

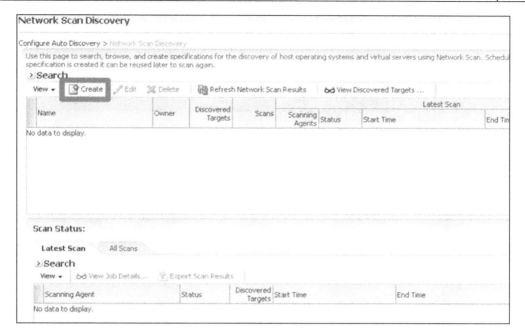

4. Select the agent you want to use to perform the IP scan. You will need to specify the IP ranges for each agent. You can set a hostname, IP address, or and IP range:

5. You can go to the **Job Details** tab and schedule an IP scan discovery schedule. The **Host Discovery** page shows you the status of IP scan discovery processes and shows a list of OVM Managers that are found a s part of the discovery process.

Virtual Server discovery

The Oracle VM Manager uses the term "virtual server" for a physical machine that has a hypervisor running on it. The OVM Hypervisor is based on **Xen Hypervisor** and can support several types of platforms for guest VMs. A virtual server also includes an Oracle VM agent that communicates to Oracle VM Manager.

Oracle VM Servers are grouped into server pools. All members of a server pool can access shared storage (we will talk about shared storage configuration later in this chapter). NFS, SAN, or iSCSI storage can also be attached.

First, we will discover virtual servers; to do so perform the following steps:

1. Navigate to **Enterprise | Cloud | Infrastructure Home**.
2. Right-click on the target and select **Discover Virtual Servers**.

3. Specify the hostname or IP address of the virtual servers on separate lines and provide the Oracle VM Agent credentials.
4. Click on **Submit** to start the discovery.

Networking

We will need to set up and configure logical networks that will be connected to the physical network ports on OVM Servers. This is a critical piece of setup, and we suggest you make sure your physical network components (subnets, VLANs) are correctly set up. Enterprise Manager makes this step as painless as possible, but if the underlying physical interfaces are misconfigured, there is a chance that you will encounter difficulty in debugging issues. While setting up OVM Networks, we will need to do the following:

- Generate MAC addresses
- Create and configure VLAN groups
- Create logical networks

Generating MAC addresses

It is important to understand how Oracle VM Manager handles network traffic. VM Manager uses VNICs. A **Virtual Network Interface Card** (**VNIC**) is a pseudo network interface technology sitting on top of the physical network adaptor; in most cases a NIC. Each physical network interface (NIC) usually has multiple VNICs, and for a system such as Oracle VM Manager, a VNIC appears just like a physical NIC. These VNICs are assigned MAC addresses that are different from the ones assigned to physical NICs. VNICs play the role of managing physical network traffic to Virtual Machines. We will need to generate MAC addresses to assign to VNICs; to do so perform the following steps:

1. Navigate to **Enterprise | Cloud | Infrastructure Home**.
2. Right-click on an OVM Manager target and select **Manage Network**.
3. Click on the **Generate** button and specify the initial MAC address range.

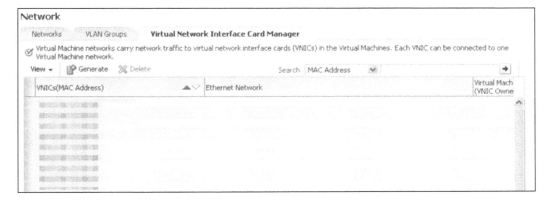

Creating and configuring VLAN groups

This step can be skipped if you are not using VLANs in your physical network. A **VLAN** is a broadcast domain created by switches. As the network grows and broadcast traffic on the network grows, using VLANs usually becomes a wise choice. As you may probably know, VLANs allow a single virtualized interface for different network interfaces across subnets. VLANs offer better performance by containing broadcast traffic over the network and by putting all devices under one network. They also provide better security. Each VLAN has a unique identifier called a **VLAN ID**. You can create VLAN groups in Oracle VM Manager by performing the following steps:

1. Navigate to **Enterprise | Cloud | Infrastructure Home**.
2. Right-click on the OVM Manager target and click on **Manager Networks**.
3. Click on the **Create** button in the **VLAN** tab.
4. Enter a value for the **VLAN Segments** in the range of 1 to 4094. This is the identifier we talked about earlier.
5. When you click on **Add**, you can select ports to be added to the network and one or more virtual servers.

Creating networks

A network is a group of virtual server physical NIC ports. We will create a network using Oracle VM Manager.

1. Navigate to **Enterprise | Cloud | Infrastructure Home**.
2. Right-click on the OVM Manager target and click on **Manager Networks**.
3. In the **Networks** tab, click on the **Create** option. You will have the option to configure ports for VLAN groups we created earlier. You can either configure VLAN groups or go ahead without that step. We already saw how to create and configure VLAN groups earlier, so we will go ahead by clicking on **Continue Network Creation**.

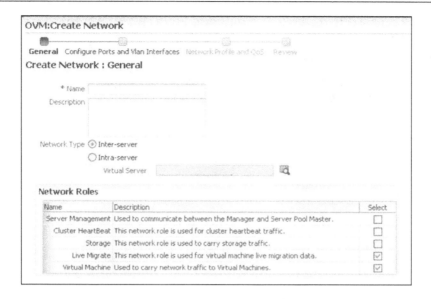

4. Specify the network type—**Inter-server** networks allow server-to-server communication and allow traffic to be routed via standard switches while **Intra-server** networks don't allow traffic to be routed to an external network.

5. In the **Network Roles** table, select the appropriate checkbox to assign roles. **Network Roles** or **Channels** allow us to create separate networks specific to a use case and direct traffic for each role. Oracle VM Manager determines what kind of traffic is handled by which network, based on these roles. Oracle VM Manager has the following categories of roles:

   ° **Server Management**: When this role is assigned to a network, Oracle VM Manager will allow IP addresses to be assigned to physical interfaces on VM servers. This means that Oracle VM Manager will be able to communicate with agents via physical VM servers.

   ° **Cluster Heartbeat**: This is not very useful unless you are using Oracle Cluster Filesystem2. This role will enable the network to send heartbeat messages to verify if VM Servers are running.

   ° **Storage**: This role can be used to enable any network port for network traffic on NFS or iSCSI. Again, this role is not widely used.

   ° **Live Migrate**: This role is useful while migrating VMs from one virtual server to another in a server pool.

   ° **Virtual Machine**: This role allows traffic between Guest VMs in the server pool and also between guests and external network. While creating a network, make sure we can support Guest VMs, and then select the **Virtual Machine** role.

6. Click on **Next** to navigate to **Configure Ports** and **VLAN Interfaces** steps. You can add a VLAN group from the list.

7. Click on **Add** and select the ports you want to be added to the network.

8. Clicking on **Next** will show an option step to configure **Network profile and QoS**, as shown in the following screenshot:

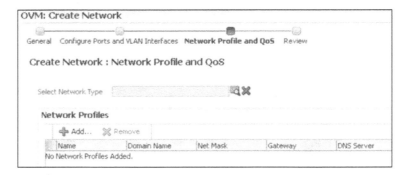

9. You can select the network type from the following: **Internet Routable** (network can be routed through the Internet), **Non-internet Routable**, and **RFC1918** (cannot be routed through the Internet and must use a predefined set of private IP addresses).

10. You can also add network profiles. Network profiles are used to automatically assign IP addresses and common networking parameters to guest VMs. Network profiles make it easy to manage guest VMs. Before we can add network profiles, let's see how we can create them.

Creating a network profile

Perform the following steps to create a network profile:

1. Navigate to **Setup** | **Provisioning and Patching** | **Network Profile**, and click on **Create**.

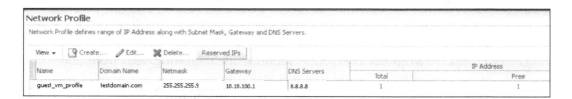

2. Enter values for **Domain Name** in the format `testdomain.com`, a network mask, gateway, and a DNS server.

3. You can either specify a list of IPs or a range of IP addresses. If you choose to specify a list, you can enter a list of hostname and MAC address combinations, and if you choose to give a range of IPs, an IP address range start value is appended to the host name (for example, if the hostname pattern is `testhostname` **and we start the range with** `1.`**, the first IP address would be something like** `10.1.1.1` **and last IP address would be** `10.1.1.4`**; the resulting hostnames would look** like `testhostname1`, `testhostname2`, `testhostname3`, and `testhostname4`).

Configuring storage servers

The other important aspect for setting up an Infrastructure as a Service is **shared storage**. Virtual servers inside the server pool use shared storage mounted on external storage servers, filesystems, or LUNs. These external storage servers are available for the virtual servers via fiber channels or network communication over Ethernet.

Oracle VM Manager makes use of both standard and vendor-specific plugins to support almost all flavors of storage:

*   **Local Storage**: This uses the local hard disks on Oracle VM Servers. This option is not used on most real-life use cases. When the topology becomes more complex and you start thinking about HA (high availability), using replication and clustering, you will immediately realize the limitations of local storage for VMs.

*   **Network Attached Storage (NAS)**: This is typically on NFS. **Network file system** (**NFS**) is an industry standard filesystem and can allow shared storage to VMs inside the server pool. NFS allows for flexible clustering and HA configuration. NFS storage can be discovered via hostnames or IP addresses.

*   **Storage Attached Network (SAN)**: This storage can be either iSCSI or Fiber Channel. Neither differs much in terms of the functionalities they offer. Most modern storage vendors provide iSCSI, and it's getting wider industry acceptance. However, vendor-specific plugins are required for specialized operations on the iSCSI storage (extending LUNs, Cloning, and so on).

To setup storage servers, perform the following steps:

1. Navigate to **Enterprise | Cloud | Infrastructure Home**. Select **Manager Storage** after right-clicking on the OVM target.

2. You will see a list of file servers, storage arrays, and local file servers. You can click on the link indicating the type of storage to register a file server or storage array.

3. Also, you can select a storage element type and click on **Discover**. OVM Manager will discover the available filesystem of the selected type and refresh this page.

4. You can click on **Validate** after selecting an element to validate the storage system for connectivity issues and other issues like volume out of space and misaligned LUNs.

Registering a file server

Perform the following steps to register a file server:

1. On the storage page, click on the **File Server** link for the storage type element you want to register a file server for:

2. As we discussed earlier, Oracle VM Manager uses standardized default plugins and vendor-specific plugins to provide access to various sources of storage systems. The standard set of plugins provides all necessary basic connectivity, but if you want to avail yourself of the specialized features for a storage system, you can install the vendor-specific plugin. Those plugins are listed in this screen under drop-down box **Plugin Name**. Select the right type of plugin for the storage you are trying to configure here.

3. Enter **Admin host**, **Username**, and **Password** values. These are the values related to the administration host for Oracle VM Manager. **Access Host** is the host IP or hostname for the external storage system host.

4. **Uniform Exports** allows you to have all VM servers in the server pool share the same NFS exports. This is usually the preferred configuration when you don't need multiple NFS exports within one server pool for a single storage system.

5. When you finish this process and come back to the **Storage Details** page, you can see the newly registered file server once you finish the discovery process by clicking on the **Discover** button.

Registering the storage array

Perform the following steps to register a storage array:

1. You can click on the link specifying the storage array type on the storage page. You will see the first step of the process to register a storage array:

2. On this page, you can select the **Storage Type**. As we discussed earlier, you can select either **Fiber Channel** or **iSCSI Storage Array** type.

3. **Plugin Name** allows you to select either the generic-storage plugin or a vendor-specific plugin. **Plugin Private Data** is applicable only for vendor-specific plugins where the external plugin might want a set of configuration values.

4. Clicking on **Next** on this page will take you to the next screen of this process where you can enter access information:

5. You can enter the **Access Host** and **Access Port** values of the external storage system.

6. When you finish this process and come back to the **Storage Details** page, you can see the newly registered file server once you finish the discovery process by clicking on the **Discover** button.

Creating a storage repository

A **storage repository** is a logical place where VM artifacts and resources (VM templates, VM configuration files, ISO or DVD images for VMs, and so on) will reside. You can think of storage repository as a logical disk abstracted out of the physical storage. Let's see how we can create a storage repository for the server pool:

1. Navigate to **Enterprise | Cloud | Infrastructure Home**.

2. Right-click on **OVM Target** and click on **Manage Storage Repository**.

3. Click on the **Create** button. In the resulting pop up, search for the storage server and the file system on which you want the storage repository to be created. You can provide a value for **Share Path** for the NFS storage type:

Presenting storage repositories

Once the storage repository is created, it's time to promote it to a server pool. This process is called "presenting" of storage repository. Typically, all of the virtual servers are presented with the storage repository.

1. Navigate to **Enterprise | Cloud | Infrastructure Home**.

2. Right-click on **OVM Target** and click on **Manage Storage Repository**.

3. Select the storage repository from the drop-down list; you will be able to see all the server pools on which storage repositories have been propagated.

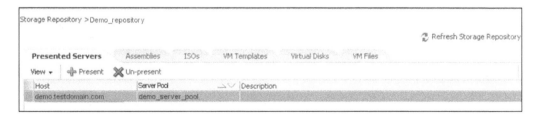

4. Select the server pool from the list and click on **Present**.

5. Click on the **Select Servers** icon and expand the members listed in the dialog. You will need to select the checkboxes for zones, pools, or individual virtual servers in the resulting dialog.

6. Click on **Present** to mount the selected members from the earlier screens.

Creating and configuring virtual server pools

A **virtual server pool** is essentially a container of one or more virtual machines or guest VMs. Server pools allow shared storage access for all the VMs and seamlessly balances the load across resources. You will, of course, need to supply enough physical resources to support the number of VMs within the server pool. Luckily, server pools can scale easily by just adding more physical resources. Let's discuss how we can create server pools:

1. Navigate to **Enterprise | Cloud | Infrastructure Home**.

2. Right-click on the OVM Target and click on **Create Virtual Server Pool**; you will be greeted with an elaborate screen:

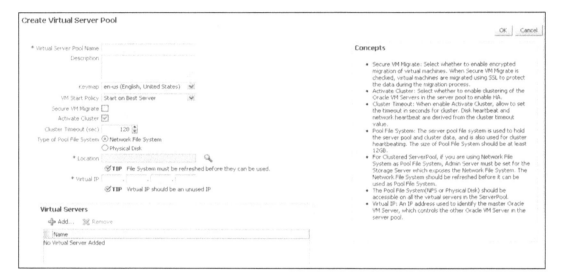

3. **The VM Start Policy** field allows you to decide how you want a VM to start. You can chose **Start on Best Server** to let Oracle VM Manager select the best server (at that point of time when VM is booted) for the VM to start. Alternatively, you can select **Start on Current Server** and the VM will be started on the server that created the VM.

4. Selecting **Secure VM Migrate** will let you migrate virtual machines using SSL to add more security while data is migrated.

5. Selecting **Active Cluster** enables HA pairing on the server pool. HA clusters are a group of machines where redundant servers continue to serve the application even if any of the servers fail. Most of the time, Active/Active or Active/Passive configuration is used. For more information on VM High Availability, check the documentation at `http://www.oracle.com/us/technologies/026966.pdf`.

6. You can select the type of filesystem that will be used to contain the server pool and cluster-related data for HA (if enabled). You can select either **NFS** or **Physical Disk**. As we discussed earlier, for all practical purposes, using a shared storage mount such as NFS is advisable for containing virtual servers.

7. You can click on the **Location** search icon to discover the filesystem location depending on the type of filesystem you have selected earlier.

8. **Virtual IP** is an IP address of the master server in the server pool.

Monitoring and administering IaaS

Oracle Enterprise Manager offers a comprehensive management console where you can perform administration and monitoring of your cloud infrastructure. In this section, we will be focusing on how to utilize the Oracle Enterprise Manager Infrastructure Cloud Home and perform various administrative tasks.

Most of the tasks that you will be concerned with are performed either on Infrastructure Cloud Home, Oracle VM Manager Home, or Virtual Server Pool Home page. We will look at each of these portals in this section.

The Infrastructure Cloud Home page

Navigate to **Enterprise** | **Cloud** | **Infrastructure Home**. The **Infrastructure Cloud Home** page shows several valuable details under different navigation panes:

- **General**: Displays a count and status of OVM Managers, zones, guest VMs, and servers.

- **Target Flux**: This pane displays the number of targets created and deleted over the last month (30 days). Targets included in this graph are guest VMs, virtual servers, server pools, and VM Managers.

- **Request Status**: This shows a list of requests and their statuses:

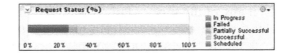

- **CPU and Memory Status**: This pane gives an overview of percentage utilization of compute resources like CPU and memory.

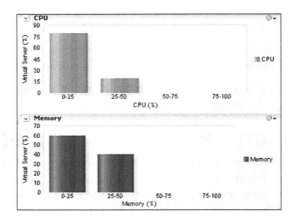

- **Inventory and Usage**: This pane shows server pools, virtual servers, and guest VMs. You can select the value from the dropdown, and the corresponding list will show artifacts under the group. For example, select **Oracle VM Guests** from under the **Show** dropdown to show a list of guest VMs under the Oracle VM Manager:

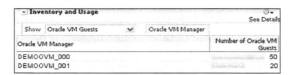

The Oracle Virtual Machine Manager home page

OVM Manager home page is a dashboard with a set of widgets showing information about virtual servers, zones (set of server pools), server pools, and guest VMs.

Navigate to **Enterprise | Cloud | Infrastructure Home**, and on left-hand side pane, click on a target. OVM Manager home page shows the following information:

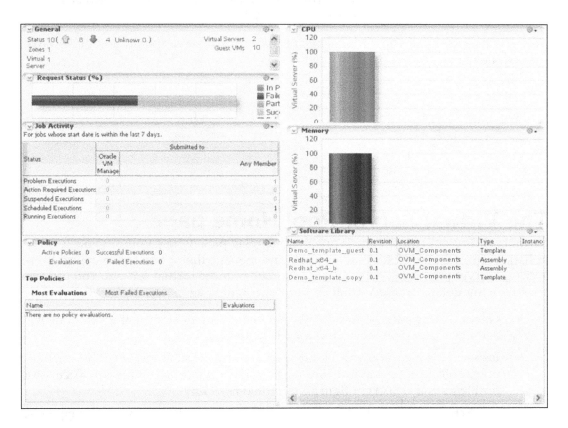

- **General**: This shows a list of OVM Manager artifacts and their statuses
- **Job Activity**: This shows a list of all requests processed by OVM Manager and their status over the period of 1 week
- **Software Library**: This shows all the templates and assemblies that got deployed in the OVM Manager

We can perform quite a lot of administration tasks via OVM Manager. We will now go through some important ones.

View and manage virtualization targets

Navigate to **Enterprise | Cloud | Infrastructure Home**, right click on **Infrastructure Cloud**, select **Members** and then select **Show All**.

You can see a list of all OVM Managers, virtual servers, server pools, and guest VMs that can be managed.

The Virtual Server Pool Home page

Virtual Server Pool Home Page is one more display pane where you can take a holistic view of all the virtual server pools and manage them. You will recollect that a virtual server pool is a logical collection of one or more virtual servers. You can see the following details on the Virtual Server Pool Home Page:

- **General**: This pane shows details of a virtual server such as the VM Zone it belongs to, total memory, and total disk space.

- **Issues**: This pane shows all issues reported by member targets of this virtual pool. This information is useful when you want to track commonly occurring problems and detect configuration problems, if any.

- **Job Activity**: This pane shows all the jobs launched during the last seven days.

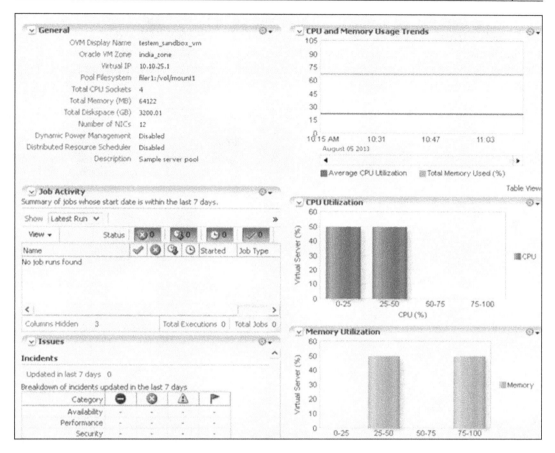

Till now, we talked about Virtual Server Pool Home Page. As virtual server pools are a logical group of virtual servers, it is important to understand how to manage virtual servers. Luckily, Oracle VM Manager provides a dashboard named Virtual Server Home Page to monitor and manage all the virtual servers inside a virtual server pool.

Virtual servers are physical machines where hypervisors are running. Virtual servers belong to only one virtual server pool.

We will see how we can manage virtual servers from Virtual Server Home Page. To launch Virtual Server Home Page, navigate to **Enterprise | Cloud | Infrastructure Home** and select the virtual server from the left-hand side pane. Once selected, the main (center) panel will refresh with the detailed page related to the selected virtual server.

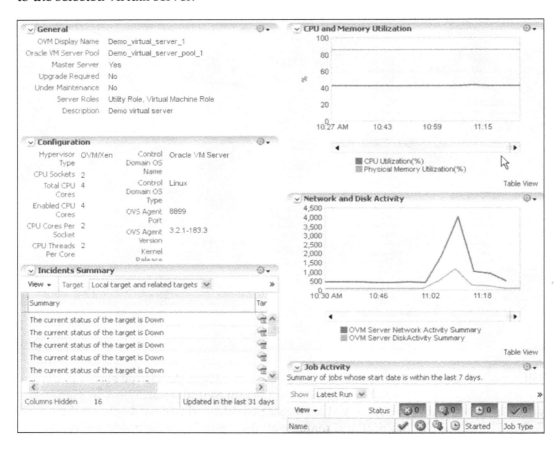

This page shows you a lot of information about the virtual server. You can track the network and disk activity and the CPU utilization trends. You can also review and fix incidents reported in this dashboard. We will see how you can manage virtual servers from here.

Editing virtual servers

From the Virtual Server Home Page, navigate to **Virtual Server | Target Setup | Edit VM Server**. This screen allows you to edit not only the description but also a few other attributes of the virtual server.

Configure **Intelligent Platform Management Interface (IPMI)** by selecting the **Enable IPMI** checkbox. This option allows you to shut down a VM remotely and send a wake-on to LAN message to power-on the VM without any physical intervention. This is usually a good option to have.

You can either select **Utility Role** or **Virtual Machine Role** for the virtual machine to perform. **Utility Role** is designated for administrative tasks (for example, creating or deleting assemblies, cloning VMs, and importing templates). The **Virtual Machine** role, on the other hand, marks a server to be used as a VM.

Maintaining a virtual server

Occasionally, you will need to put a virtual server into maintenance mode while you upgrade or replace hardware or software components. Usually, maintenance tasks are planned and users are informed to save their work and shut down their VMs in advance. Sometimes, for emergency maintenance, administrators need to put the virtual server in maintenance mode without much preplanning. When a virtual server is put into maintenance mode, all VMs running on it are transferred seamlessly to other virtual servers in the server pool. If there are no virtual servers left in the pool, the VMs are stopped.

You can put the virtual server into maintenance mode as follows:

1. Navigate to **Enterprise | Cloud | Infrastructure Home** and select virtual server from the left-hand side panel.
2. Right-click on the virtual server and select **Start Maintenance**.
3. You can click on **Stop Maintenance** to let the virtual server join the server pool again and be operational.

Setting up the IaaS self-service portal

We have covered quite a bit of ground in setting up a scalable IaaS. We discussed earlier how IaaS's real power is in the way users can utilize the resources via self-service portals. Self-service provisioning is the reason why most enterprises invest in IaaS, as it greatly reduces maintenance and administration costs. In the remaining part of this chapter, we will continue to understand the overall IaaS configuration using Oracle Enterprise Manager and will discuss how we can set up a self-service model using Oracle Enterprise Manager.

The self-service model allows the administrators to manage several routine configurations easily. Administrators can manage VM images, user quotas, compute, and storage resources for server pools and so on.

Let us take a detailed look at steps to set up and configure an IaaS self-service portal.

Setting up machine sizes

You can customize and configure various machine sizes you are going to offer for provisioning VMs.

Navigate to **Setup** | **Cloud** | **Infrastructure** and click on **Machine Sizes**.

Default sizes of small, medium, and large are preconfigured for you and you can create new machine sizes from this screen.

Machine sizes are usually determined based on the type of workload you intend to assign to those machines. For production servers you may choose large servers, while for load test machines, small servers might be sufficient. For background tasks, a small machine is recommended, but for real-time applications, you might need a medium or large server. As cost is directly proportional to the size of the machine, choosing the correct size is critical:

You can click on the **Create** button to create new machine sizes or right-click on the existing machine sizes and edit them.

Modify provisioning request settings

You can click on **Request Settings** on the left-hand pane to edit provisioning request and reservation details:

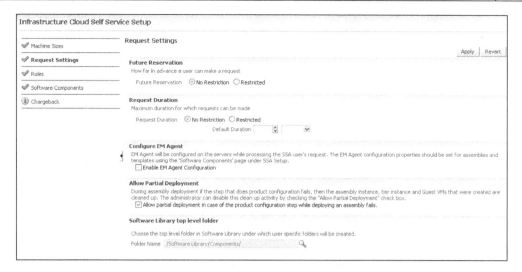

You can change the following values:

- **Future Reservations**: This allows or disallows users from requests to provision resources in advance by selecting the appropriate radio button.

- **Request Duration**: This controls the duration for which provision requests can be made.

- **Allow Partial Deployment**: You can enable this option by selecting the checkbox. If you allow partial deployment, guest VMs and assembly instances will *not* get cleared off if product deployment fails.

Modifying roles

Roles are used to assign a set of privileges and quotas to a group of users. These roles can be configured to have more fine-grained controls on resource provisioning.

Click on **Roles** from the left-hand panel, and in the **Roles Details** page, you can modify the quota assignments within this screen:

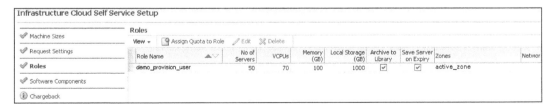

Click on the **Assign Quota to Role** button and you will be able to assign a quota to the particular role or modify the current assignment. Click on the **Select Role** search icon and select the role you want to modify. Similarly, click on the **Select Zone** icon to select the zone from the list.

You will be able to modify the following values:

- You can define the number of servers that a user can reserve at one time. One thing to notice here is the total number of servers across zones.

- Apart from the number of servers, you can set the number of Virtual CPUs (VCPU), the maximum memory allocation, and the maximum disk sizes.

Modifying software components

You can make templates and assemblies available to the self-service portal users. Click on the **Software Components** option on the left-hand side panel to open the software components details page:

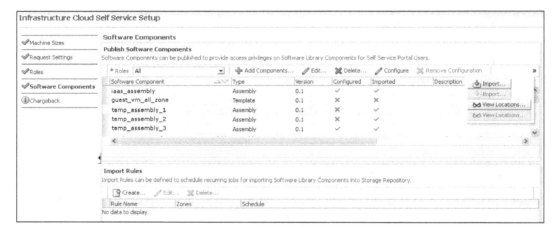

You can add new software components by clicking on the **Add Components** button. Inside the resulting page (**Publish Assemblies/Templates**), you can add assemblies or templates in the following manner:

1. Click on the **Add** button and add the assembly or template from the list.

2. Click on the **Add** button and add the role from the list.

3. Finally, publish the changes by clicking on **Publish**.

Summary

We have covered quite a bit of ground in understanding the possibilities for creating a scalable Infrastructure as a Service environment. We went through various building blocks of IaaS and we reviewed all the necessary configuration options on Oracle Enterprise Manager. A successful implementation of IaaS requires careful planning and proper estimates of scale. We will talk about another implementation model of Database as a Service in the next chapter. We will also take a look at the various chargeback options available.

Database as a Service

3

We saw how a robust IaaS infrastructure can be deployed using Oracle Enterprise Manager. IaaS acts as the backbone for higher level cloud computing implementations — **Platform as a Service (PaaS)** and **Software as a Service (SaaS)**. Platform as a Service is a very interesting take on the traditional cloud computing models. While there are many (often conflicting) definitions of a PaaS, for all practical purposes, PaaS provides a complete platform and environment to build and host applications or services. Emphasis is clearly on providing an end-to-end precreated environment to develop and deploy the application that automatically scales as required. PaaS packs together all the necessary components such as an operating system, database, programming language, libraries, web or application container, and a storage or hosting option. PaaS offerings vary and their chargebacks are dependent on what is utilized by the end user. There are excellent public offerings of PaaS such as Google App Engine, Heroku, Microsoft Azure, and Amazon Elastic Beanstalk. In a private cloud offering for an enterprise, it is possible to implement a similar PaaS environment. Out of the various possibilities, we will focus on building a **Database as a Service (DBaaS)** infrastructure using Oracle Enterprise Manager. DBaaS is sometimes seen as a mix of PaaS or SaaS depending on the kind of service it provides. DBaaS that provides services such as a database would be leaning more towards its PaaS legacy; but if it provides a service such as Business Intelligence, it takes more of a SaaS form.

Oracle Enterprise Manager enables self-service provisioning of virtualized database instances out of a common shared database instance or cluster. Oracle Database is built to be clustered, and this makes it an easy fit for a robust DBaaS platform.

The topics covered in this chapter are as follows:

- Setting up the PaaS infrastructure
- Provisioning the database
- Managing storage servers

- Creating database pools
- Setting up quotas and provisioning profiles
- Setting up service templates and chargebacks

Setting up the PaaS infrastructure

Before we go about implementing a DBaaS, we will need to make sure our common platform is up and working.

We have already discussed how we can automatically monitor or manually add hosts to Enterprise Manager; we will now check how we can create a PaaS Zone.

Creating PaaS Zones

Enterprise Manager groups host or Oracle VM Manager Zones into **PaaS Infrastructure Zones**. You will need to have at least one PaaS Zone before you can add more features into the setup. To create a PaaS Zone, make sure that you have the following:

- The `EM_CLOUD_ADMINISTRATOR`, `EM_SSA_ADMINISTRATOR`, and `EM_SSA_USER` roles created
- A software library

To set up a PaaS Infrastructure Zone, perform the following steps:

1. Navigate to **Setup** | **Cloud** | **PaaS Infrastructure Zone**.
2. Click on **Create** in the **PaaS Infrastructure Zone** main page.

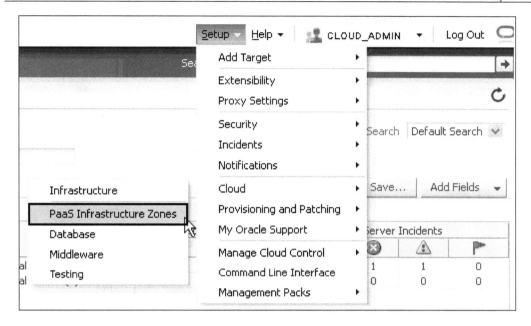

3. Enter the necessary details for **PaaS Infrastructure Zone** such as **Name** and **Description**.

4. Based on the type of members you want to add to this zone, you can select any of the following member types:

   ◦ **Host**: This option will only allow the host targets to be part of this zone. Also, make sure you provide the necessary details for the placement policy constraints defined per host. These values are used to prevent over utilization of hosts which are already being heavily used.
   You can set a percentage threshold for Maximum CPU Utilization and Maximum Memory Allocation. Any host exceeding this threshold will not be used for provisioning.

○ **OVM Zone**: This option will allow you to add Oracle Virtual Manager Zone targets:

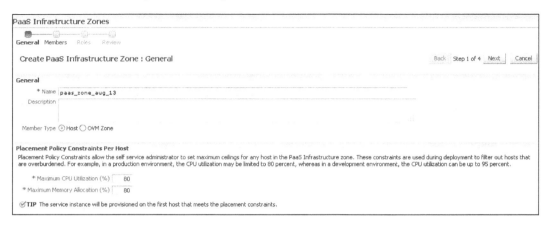

5. If you select **Host** at this stage, you will see the following page:

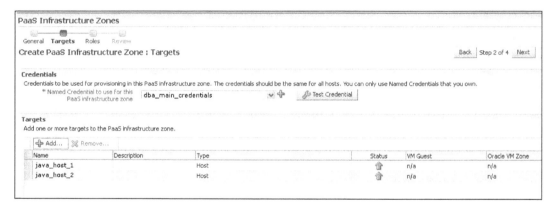

6. Click on the **+** button to add named credentials and make sure you click on **Test Credentials** button to verify the credential. These named credentials must be global and available on all the hosts in this zone.

7. Click on the **Add** button to add target hosts to this zone.

8. If you selected **OVM Zone** in the previous screen (step 1 of 4), you will be presented with the following screen:

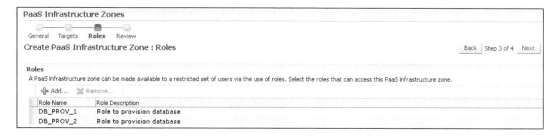

9. Click on the **Add** button to add roles that can access this PaaS Infrastructure Zone.

Once you have created a PaaS Infrastructure Zone, you can proceed with setting up necessary pieces for a DBaaS. However, time and again you might want to edit or review your Paas Infrastructure Zone.

1. To view and manage your PaaS Infrastructure Zones, navigate to **Enterprise Menu | Cloud | Middleware and Database Cloud | PaaS Infrastructure Zones**.

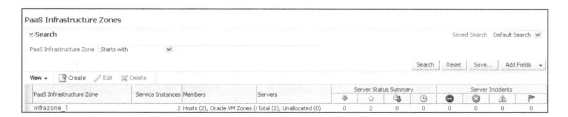

2. From this page you can create, edit, delete, or view more details for a PaaS Infrastructure Zone. Clicking on the PaaS infrastructure zone link will display a detailed drill-down page with quite a few details related to that zone. The page is shown as follows:

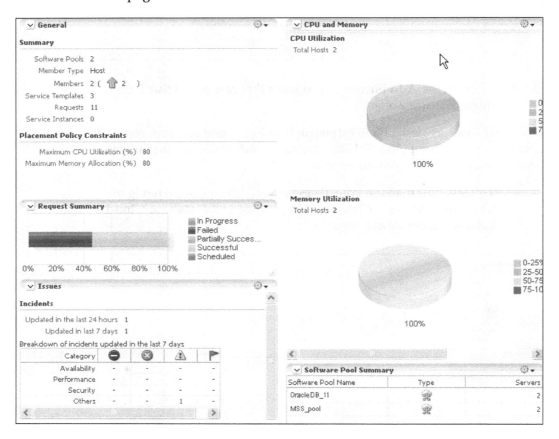

This page shows a lot of very useful details about the zone. Some of them are listed as follows:

- **General**: This section shows stats for this zone and shows details such as the total number of software pools, Oracle VM zones, member types (hosts or Oracle VM Zones), and other related details.

- **CPU and Memory**: This section gives an overview of CPU and memory utilization across all servers in the zone.

- **Issues**: This section shows incidents and problems for the target. This is a handy summary to check if there are any issues that needs attention.

- **Request Summary**: This section shows the status of requests being processed currently.

- **Software Pool Summary**: This section shows the name and type of each software pool in the zone.

- **Unallocated Servers**: This section shows a list of servers that are not associated with any software pool.

- **Members**: This section shows the members of the selected zones.

- **Service Template Summary**: Shows the service templates associated with the zone.

Provisioning the database

The first step in building a DBaaS environment is to provision the database software and make sure the provisioned database instances are available on all hosts. There are the following two methods of provisioning databases in Oracle Enterprise Manager:

- **Using provisioning profiles**: You can create provisioning profiles and use the database image from these profiles to provision database instances. This process makes sure that you have all the necessary templates and plugins as part of the deployment. You can create a provisioning profile by navigating to **Enterprise | Provisioning and Patching | Database Provisioning**.

- **Using installer**: This method involves installing plugins manually and running the database installer to set up the cluster and install the database program:

  1. To deploy database plugins to the agents in the current PaaS Infrastructure Zone, navigate to **Setup | Extensibility | Plugins**.
  2. Run Clusterware/ASM installer to set up the cluster and ASM.
  3. Run the database installer to install and create a database.
  4. To discover the newly installed database, navigate to **Setup | Add Target | Add Targets Manually | Add Non-Host Targets using Guided Process**.

Managing storage servers

In this section we will discuss how we can configure underlying storage systems such as NetApp Storage System or Sun ZFS Storage to host our database instances. Naturally, our shared database instance will require storage to host the data, and when the user wants to provision an instance of a database, Oracle Enterprise Manager provisions the preconfigured slice of underlying storage space to host that database instance. We will check how we can configure and register various storage systems for Oracle Enterprise Manager. As of Oracle Enterprise Manager Cloud Control 12*c*, only NetApp and Sun ZFS storage is supported. We will discuss the configuration of both systems.

When we register the storage inside Oracle Enterprise Manager, we can utilize snapshot management and cloning functionalities supported by these storage systems. Oracle Enterprise Manager can quickly create exact replicas of database instances using a technology called SnapClone. **SnapClone** uses the underlying storage system's cloning functionalities and provides very how we can configure underlying storage systems such as efficient copy-on-write cloning of database instances.

When we have to manage many database instances, SnapClone can come in very handy when rapidly cloning and provisioning golden images for the database templates.

Configuring NetApp or Sun ZFS servers involves obtaining licenses specific to the vendor and assigning specific storage capabilities. These processes are very vendor-specific and hence we will not go into details of this process. Make sure you go through the documentation for the specific storage vendor to understand which privileges are required to be configured.

Registering storage servers

Once you have registered storage servers by adding necessary vendor libraries and configuring privileges, we can register the storage servers to Oracle Enterprise Manager. To register a storage server, perform the following steps:

1. Navigate to **Setup | Provisioning and Patching | Storage Registration**.

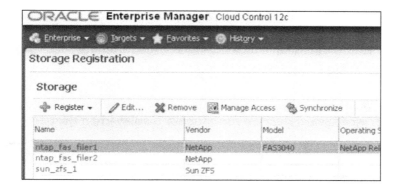

Remember that you will need the role EM_STORAGE_ADMINISTRATOR to administer the storage servers.

2. Click on **Register** and select either the **NetApp Storage** or **Sun ZFS Storage** option.

3. In the resulting screen, enter protocol (**http** or **https**) and storage credentials for the storage system:

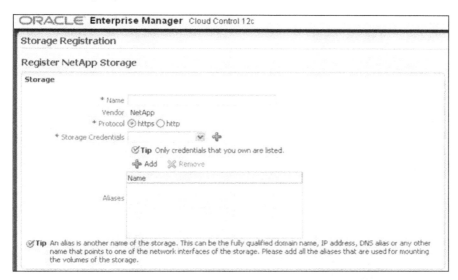

Optionally you can enter storage aliases. These aliases can be a fully qualified domain name, DNS alias, or an IP address. These aliases are very critical in discovering correct mount points.

4. Let's say you have a NetApp storage system named `myNetAppFiler.com`. The same system has an alias named `myNetAppFilerAlias.com`. If your database instance uses an aliased mount point such as `myNetAppFilerAlias.com:/root_vol/`, you must add the alias while registering the storage.

5. In the **Agent to Manage Storage** step, click on **Add** to add a management host. You can select the host from the list displayed on the page:

6. In the resulting screen you can add storage by searching for them in the **Search** dialog as displayed in the following screenshot:

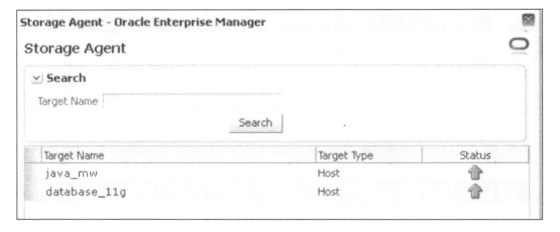

Synchronizing storage servers

When you click on the **Submit** button to register a storage server, a background job is run to synchronize the newly registered storage server. When any of the parameters are changed on the storage server, such as when a new **logical unit number (LUN)** is mapped, you will need to run this job manually to synchronize those changed parameters. If you are manually running this job, make sure you are not running it during a peak usage time and try to schedule the job when there are few or no SnapClone jobs running. To manually schedule synchronization, perform the following steps:

1. Navigate to the **Storage Registration** page and click on **Synchronize**.

2. Click on **OK** on the confirmation page. This will launch the background job. You can monitor the status of the job by checking the synchronization status of the agent on the **Storage Registration** page:

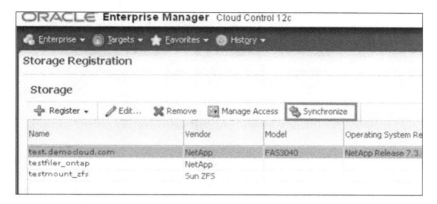

3. By default, the synchronization is scheduled to run every 3 hours. If you need to change it, you can click on the **Edit** button on the **Storage Registration** page for the particular storage. In the **Edit Storage** page, you can edit the repetition time and frequency.

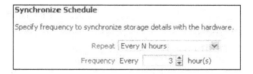

We have covered quite a few important milestones in setting up DBaaS using Oracle Enterprise Manager. In the remaining part of this chapter, we will take a look at setting up a self-service solution for DBaaS where users can provision, manage, and monitor their database instances.

Creating database pools

The first thing we will look at is how we can create a database pool. A **database pool** is a collection of targets (servers or clusters) with a database image installed. Database pools are used to provision database instances within PaaS Infrastructure Zones.

To create a database pool, you will need to log in to Oracle Enterprise Manager using the EM_SSA_ADMINISTRATOR role. Once logged in, you can navigate to **Setup | Cloud | Database**. From the **Database Cloud Self Service Portal Setup** page, click on

Create and select **For Database**:

You will need to enter a few details in this page. Some important fields are as follows:

- **Credentials**: You will need to provide the host credentials for database creation. If you are using a thinly-provisioned storage, you will need to provide root credentials for the storage system.

- **Oracle Homes**: You will need to enter appropriate values for **PaaS Infrastructure Zone**, **Database Configuration** (single instance of RAC), **Platform** (Linux x86-x64), and **Version** (11.2.0.3.0) of the database being deployed. You can add these Oracle Homes by clicking on the **Add** button.

- **Maximum Number of Database Instances per Host**: This is an upper limit for resource utilization that helps you manage the resource consumption for each database host.

When you allow self-provisioning of database instances, it's always advisable to control the provisioning so that there is something for everyone. By controlling the provisioning we are not consuming huge resources on a few requests, instead, we are leaving the larger user base waiting for more.

Although there is no universal solution for achieving the best possible provisioning policy, we can use certain features of Oracle Enterprise Manager to control and distribute the provisioning requests. We will briefly talk about how to configure the requests and set up quotas for users.

Oracle Enterprise Manager lets you configure when a provisioning request can be made, what should be the reservation settings for such requests, and other such settings. These settings allow you to streamline the provisioning requests.

To tweak the request configurations, navigate to **Setup | Cloud | Database** and click on the **Request Settings** tab. You can specify the following settings there:

- **Request Archive Retention**: This option specifies the period after which Enterprise Manager automatically archives the requests. You can set this option to the following:

    ◦ **No Restriction**: Requests are not archived.

    ◦ **Restricted Retention**: Archive requests older (based on a request's last modified date) than the specified duration. For example, if a request was created on Sep 1, 2013, and the restricted retention period was kept for 10 days, the retention period will be calculated based on the request's last modified date. If there were child requests that got triggered on Sep 2, Sep 4, and Sep 20, the period of retention will be calculated from Sep 20.

- **Future Reservation Length**: This option allows you to specify the period during which advance requests can be scheduled. You can set this option to the following:

    ◦ **No Restriction**: Allows you to schedule a new provision request any date later than the current date.

    ◦ **Restricted Reservation**: This option allows you to schedule the request during a specific period in the future. For example, if you set this duration to 1 year on Sep 1, 2013, future requests can be scheduled on or before Sep 1, 2014.

- **Default Retirement Period**: This option allows you to set a fixed period up to which the instance can be retained. This is the maximum time period, and an instance can be retired before this period expires. You can set values to the following:

    ◦ **No Restriction**: No end date to the instance, it can be retained as long as desired.

    ◦ **Restricted Duration**: Maximum period after which the instance needs to be retired.

Apart from tweaking the request settings, we can configure quotas to make sure we are not overutilizing our resources. A **quota** is a limit of resources that can be assigned to a provisioned database instance or role. Quotas can represent memory, storage, number of database requests, and other resource parameters.

To configure quotas, navigate to **Setup | Cloud | Database**, click on the **Quotas** tab, and then click on the **Create** button.

On the **Create New Quota** page, you can select any role that has the EM_SSA_USER privilege and create a new quota for that role. Once you select the role for the quota, you can set the following parameters:

- **Storage**: The total storage capacity that can be allocated to the database for a user under this role
- **Memory**: The total memory that can be allocated to the database for a user under this role
- **Number of Database Requests**: Sets a maximum number of database instances that can be requested by a user under this role
- **Number of Schema Service Requests**: Sets a maximum number of schemas/database services that can be requested by a user under this role

One important thing to remember is that if the user has more than one role with different quotas assigned, the overall effective quota is determined based on the entire quota combined and calculated as the maximum across roles.

For example, suppose that a user has the following roles:

- **Development Role** : Storage 15 GB, RAM 2 GB
- **QA Role**: Storage 10 GB, RAM 1 GB
- **Load Test Role**: Storage 5 GB, RAM 2 GB

This user's quota will be based on the maximum across roles and hence will be calculated as Storage: 15 GB and RAM 2 GB.

Setting correct quotas makes it easier for the admin to manage the overall database provisioning schemes. The biggest challenge faced by cloud admins is to make sure that a fine balance of necessary checks is in place, such that mission critical functions are always given priority. Setting the right quotas ensures that you always have enough resources to support all of your user needs.

Database service templates

Oracle Enterprise Manager offers a very useful feature to further automate the commonly repeated provisioning workflow. Let's say your organization has a software engineering department that provisions databases based on a set of project requirements. They have a fixed set of database structures, schemas, and configuration settings that they need to provision quite frequently. If this is a repeated workflow, it becomes tedious to create database instances with the exact same configuration every time a new provisioning request comes to the admin.

You can create database provisioning profiles to combine all of the necessary configuration and schema information to provision the database into a logical entity. You can use this profile to create service templates.

Service templates can be used by DBaaS self-service users to provision databases or schemas on their own. Service templates can be created using a SnapClone-based profile, RMAN backup-based profile, or a DBCA template-based profile. Given the scope of this text, we will not be able to go into the details of creating the actual database provisioning profiles using the mentioned methodologies, but we will take a detailed look at how we can use the database provisioning profiles to create database service templates.

SnapClone profile-based database service templates

You can use an existing SnapClone profile to create a service template. SnapClone snapshots usually contain existing installation replicas, so care should be taken to make sure only relevant template information is used for provisioning. To create a database service template, perform the following steps:

1. Navigate to **Setup | Cloud | Database**, click on **Profiles and Service Templates**, and from within the **Create** menu, select **For Database**. The following screenshot shows you the options available while creating a service template:

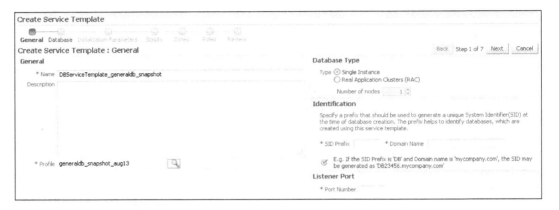

2. Provide a name and description for the template and click on the Search icon to select the SnapClone profile from the search result.

3. You can select either **Single Instance** or **RAC** database type for your template.

4. You can generate unique SIDs for the resulting database instances by setting SID prefixes. Keeping unique SIDs can help you identify the database instances at a later point in time. For example, you can keep an SID prefix of HR to identify HR instances.

5. Specify the domain name and port for the listener (specify the scan port for RAC clusters).

6. Click on **Next**.

    The resulting screen will show you all the options required to set the storage-related options for the service template:

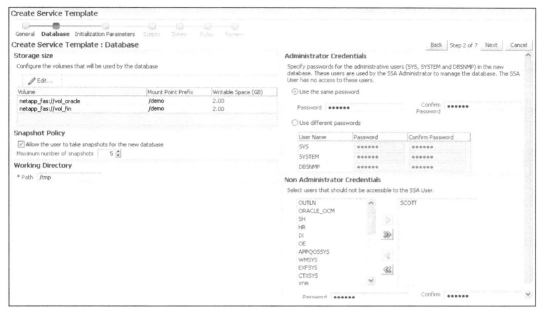

On this page, specify how the database storage will look like for this template.

7. Click on the **Edit** button in the **Storage size** pane to configure the storage volumes used by this database instance.

8. Enter the value for **Mount Point Prefix**. This prefix value is used to determine the pattern for the new mount points for the databases. Based on this pattern, new volumes will be mounted on the path that looks like the following:

```
/<mount_prefix>_<EM_generated_suffix>/<volume_source_path>
```

9. You can allow users to take snapshots of their instances by selecting the **Allow the user to take snapshots for the new database** checkbox. You can set the **Maximum number of snapshots** value to restrict the snapshot copies. These snapshots are different from the default snapshot that Oracle database maintains.

10. You will need to specify passwords for the system schemas like SYS and SYSTEM.

11. You can restrict access to some schemas for SSA User by selecting them in the **Non Administrator Credentials** region. You can assign access passwords for those schemas. The next page will let you initialize SnapClone parameters:

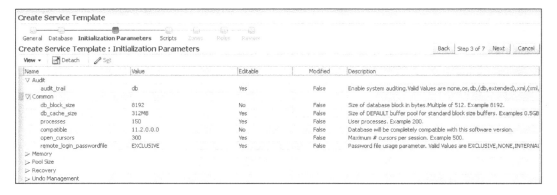

12. On this page, you have an option to modify initialization parameters. There are numerous configurations you can modify that can directly affect the way the database instance works. You can review all the default settings and click on the **Set** button to modify the editable values.

13. On the next page of the wizard, you can specify pre and post database creation script executions. If there are specific steps you want to execute before or after the database instance is created, you can specify those scripts in this screen.

14. Clicking on **Next** button will show the page where you can select a PaaS Infrastructure Zone used to provision this database instance. We can select the existing PaaS Zones in this screen:

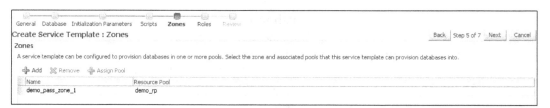

15. Click on the **Add** button to select the PaaS Zone into which the instance should be created and click on the **Assign Pool** button to select a pool to assign to the selected PaaS Zone. This will ensure that the database is provisioned into the selected pool.

16. You can restrict the availability of the service template to a specific set of roles by adding them to the template. This makes a service template more secure. Click on the **Add** button to select SSA roles. The following screenshot shows the wizard step to add a new role:

You can also create service templates using RMAN backups or DBCA template profiles. There are minor changes to those approaches from the steps we described previously.

Chargebacks

Once we have set up our PaaS model and made sure that DBaaS provisioning is working fine, it's time to think about how the resource utilization will be accounted for. All the resources we manage using our PaaS needs to be analyzed for their usage and appropriate departments or users need to be charged according to agreed upon SLA and payment terms. Chargebacks allow us to set up an elaborate matrix of usage costs and allow the admins to closely monitor the resource usage. As most PaaS implementations are self-service in nature, it becomes increasingly important and difficult to maintain correct chargebacks as per the resource utilization because there are many different types of provision requests.

Oracle Enterprise Manager lets you create very detailed chargeback mechanisms and offers excellent chargeback reports. You can set up universal as well as create granular extended chargeback plans.

We will now take a look at how you can configure chargebacks to suit your needs, but before we do that, it's worth spending some time in understanding how the chargeback mechanism works.

Oracle Enterprise Manager collects usage information from all the configured targets. You can add a virtual machine, host, database instances, Oracle VM zone, and so on. This information is extracted and transformed as part of the chargeback data collection process. Metrics can be configured based on the usage, availability, or configuration.

Chargeback targets can be added either as a dedicated mode, where usage is charged against a single cost center, or as a shared mode, where usage is charged against different cost centers.

Let's take a look at the charge plans Oracle Enterprise Manager offers. There are two types of charge plans: Universal and Extended. Universal plans are out-of-the-box plans where you can set up usage rates for metrics such as CPU, storage, and memory. Extended plans, however, allow you to modify universal plans and add custom charge points. For both types of charge plans, we will need to set the effective dates that will determine the active revision. To terminate a revision, you will need to create a new revision with effective dates, which renders the earlier revision terminated.

For example, you can create the initial revision A, with the effective date as: Jan 1, 2013 onward. You can then create a revision of that plan that has an effective date Mar 1, 2013 (effective dates for revisions are always first of a month). You can go ahead and create a few more revisions with effective dates Aug 1, 2013 and Nov 1, 2013. With this revision plan in place, we will have the following charge plans and their effective dates:

- Jan 1, 2013 to Feb 28, 2013 (first revision you created)
- Mar 1, 2013 to July 31, 2013 (second revision)
- Aug 1, 2013 to Aug 31, 2013
- Nov 1, 2013 onwards

You can view and revise only the currently active charge plan.

Creating or changing Universal charge plans

Based on the effective date of the Universal plan, you can either revise the plan or create a new plan. You will be able to select **Revision** from the **Create** menu if the effective dates are in the past and you will be able to select **Set Rates** for the plan if the effective dates are in future.

In the **Change Plan Editor** page, you can set rates and frequency for the basic metrics — **CPU**, **Storage**, and **Memory**. You can add new CPU types and add their charge rate and frequency.

Creating an Extended charge plan

In this section we will see how we can create an Extended charge plan to accommodate custom options:

1. Navigate to the **Create** menu and select **Plan**.

2. Click on **Add** to add target types to the extended plan. You can select from the list of target types.

3. Click on **Setup Configurations** and click on **Add** to open the **Add Configuration** dialog. The resulting screen will show the existing configurations, as shown in the following screenshot:

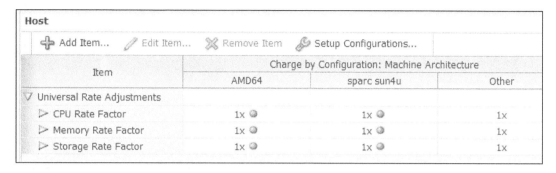

4. Click on **Add Item** to add additional charge types. You can select a charge item from the list and you can set conditions in the table itself.

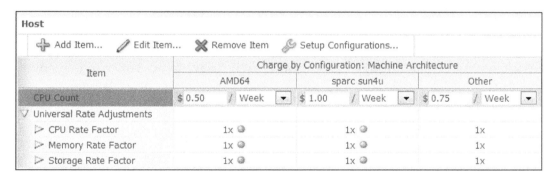

5. In the charge item row, you can specify the rate and select the frequency of charge. You can repeat this step to add several charge items. Another thing you can do is to extend the Universal charge plan. You can adjust the Universal charge items by specifying a factor of the default rate specified by the Universal charge item.

6. You can expand the rate item from the Universal charge plan and set the factor in relation to the base rate. For example, 0.5 is a decrease by 50% over the base plan.

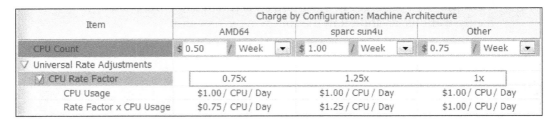

Item	Charge by Configuration: Machine Architecture		
	AMD64	sparc sun4u	Other
CPU Count	$ 0.50 / Week ▼	$ 1.00 / Week ▼	$ 0.75 / Week ▼
▽ Universal Rate Adjustments			
☑ CPU Rate Factor	0.75x	1.25x	1x
CPU Usage	$1.00 / CPU / Day	$1.00 / CPU / Day	$1.00 / CPU / Day
Rate Factor x CPU Usage	$0.75 / CPU / Day	$1.25 / CPU / Day	$1.00 / CPU / Day

7. Additionally, you will need to create and assign cost centers to targets and add the targets to the chargeback.

Once the chargeback is configured and Oracle Enterprise Manager starts capturing the usage metrics, it's important to follow the usage and chargeback trends. Let's check how useful these trends are.

Usage and charge trends

In the **Home** tab, you can check several usage trends. You can customize the view according to your requirements; you can select the time period, usage value type, resource view, or monthly aggregation view for the usage trend. For charge trends, you can customize the display for a time period, cost center, or other grouping, monthly aggregation, and so on. The following screenshot shows the usage trend over the previous week. The chart in the screenshot shows CPU, Disk space, and memory utilization:

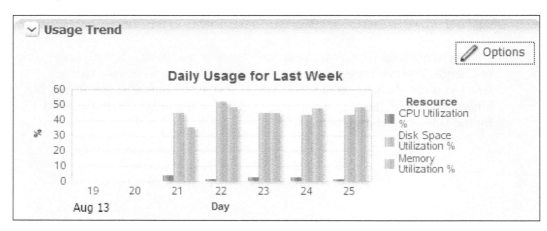

The following chart shows the trend of chargeback items:

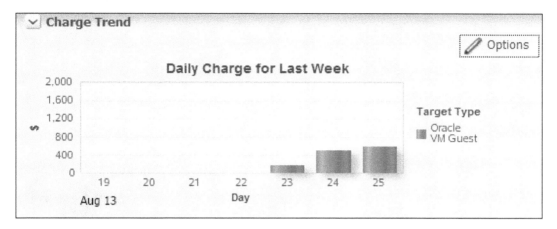

Summary

In this chapter we focused on building the Database as a Service (DBaaS) variant of a Platform as a Service (PaaS) implementation of cloud computing using Oracle Enterprise Manager. Oracle has a very strong backend database and networking technology stack and Oracle Enterprise Manager incorporates all of the components very effectively. We also saw how effectively we can use the chargeback mechanism offered by Oracle Enterprise Manager. We will discuss the comprehensive set of monitoring options in the next chapter.

4
Enterprise Monitoring

So far we have focused on building various components of cloud computing using Oracle Enterprise Manager. Like any robust system, modern cloud environments are expected to be resilient. Exceptional software engineering and system administration efforts go into making an enterprise cloud environment safe and failure proof.

However, the reality is that things will break eventually. The question is not how we can prevent failures, but how fast we can recover from failures. Cloud computing poses formidable challenges when it comes to maintaining uptime and ensuring that failures don't impact the SLAs.

Monitoring for failures or exceptional conditions is part of cloud philosophy but as the scale of the cloud grows, it gets inefficient to manually monitor the entire cloud infrastructure. Imagine a cloud environment at the scale of Amazon AWS; it would be unpractical and almost impossible to manually monitor such a cloud infrastructure. For this reason, all the scalable cloud platforms provide a very exhaustive set of automated monitoring tools.

Oracle Enterprise Manager offers a comprehensive set of tools to monitor the health and performance of your environment. Automated management agents can be configured to track specific metrics for the monitored host. When the agent finds a metric breached (for example, host going down, used memory exceeds 97 percent, or errors in database writes are high) an event is triggered and the administrator is notified of the event.

An automated monitoring and notification system is crucial for an SLA-based cloud environment to function. When the customer is charged for an uptime or performance as per the SLA, it is imperative to make sure the SLA is adhered to.

In this chapter, we will discuss the ways by which we can set up a robust automated monitoring system using Oracle Enterprise Manager.

Topics covered in this chapter:

- Monitoring concepts
- Basic setup
- Notifications
- Incident management – events, incidents, and problems

Monitoring concepts

As we discussed, Oracle Enterprise Manager comes with a very comprehensive set of metrics that can monitor health and performance of your application servers, databases, Oracle VM Manager hosts, storage, and other components that constitute the cloud environment.

You can monitor several different types of events for these components. Usually you would be interested in monitoring an exceptional event or violation of a particular parameter for a component's performance. Oracle Enterprise Manager has a set of predefined thresholds to easily set up boundaries that will raise events when breached. There are two levels of severity for the alerts raised due to such anomalies:

- **Warning**: While the threshold is breached, the component is still functional.
- **Critical**: A critical threshold is breached and the component is either not functional or very near to a failure state. These types of events will require immediate preventive action.

Based on your requirement, you should evaluate appropriate categories of the alerts. For example, you can define a warning threshold when the disk usage reaches 75 percent and raise a critical alert when the disk usage reaches 95 percent. These predefined thresholds suit most needs but it's always prudent to evaluate custom thresholds as per the SLA you are providing for your customers/organization.

Identifying correct metrics and thresholds for complex SLAs is not an easy task. Most of the times you will have to come up with a ballpark figure to baseline your thresholds but the problem here is determining what is the correct baseline? What do you measure against?

Oracle Enterprise Manager can capture the metrics over a specific period of time and prepare baselines for you. This is very useful because your estimates of the thresholds are measured against your own infrastructure's historical data and not against some arbitrary number. There are two main types of baselines periods:

- **Moving window baseline**: These baselines are drawn from a period back in time from the current date; for example, last 30 days. This is a recent evaluation of performance metrics and works well if you are interested in the recent stable performance.

- **Static baseline**: These baselines try to compare what-if workloads. For example, compare this year's end of fiscal year to previous year's end of fiscal year period.

Most practical use cases can be solved by the previous two baseline methods. These baselines let us compare estimated performance metrics with a very realistic model and it's highly recommended to use these baseline methods to evaluate your performance thresholds.

Events and actions

An alert is raised when a threshold is reached for a monitored component. This alert is an event that is triggered by the monitoring framework of Oracle Enterprise Manager. An event usually indicates a problem when a warning or critical threshold is reached. Apart from getting triggered by such thresholds, events can also be triggered by other factors, such as job execution failure, database node downtime, some critical configuration changes, and a host machine exceeding a certain percentage of CPU or memory usage. Broadly speaking, there are four major event types:

- Metric alerts like resource performance
- Availability alerts like storage resource availability
- Compliance violations like SLA violations
- Job events like status update of a scheduled job

For each of these types, you can configure alerting mechanisms differently. These even types make it easier to understand what level of corrective actions are required.

Corrective actions

Oracle Enterprise Manager lets you configure automated corrective actions for the events. These actions are triggered when the event is raised and helps ensure that the issue is resolved as soon as it is observed. Corrective actions can be a simple command to start a failing service listener or a set of tasks that can span over several hosts.

Monitoring templates

When you have a large-scale cloud environment to manage, you will observe that most of the tasks are repetitive and can be automated. The same logic applies to the kind of problems and monitoring events you want to manage. Most cloud environments have the same or similar kinds of operational problems, and with some advance planning, reaction to those problems can be automated. Oracle Enterprise Manager provides a way to standardize the monitoring parameters in a template and apply those templates to targets as required. You can define the target type for the template, metrics, thresholds, and corrective actions for the template. There are some out of the box templates provided by Oracle and there are templates certified by Oracle. Between these two, most scenarios are covered.

To list all the available templates, navigate to **Enterprise** | **Monitoring** | **Monitoring Templates**, as shown in the following screenshot:

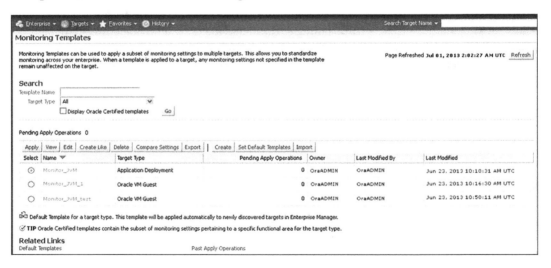

You can create, edit, or delete monitoring templates from here. To create a new monitoring template, click on the **Create** button on this screen.

You can select a target type or a specific target and the options are populated accordingly. You can add necessary values in **General**, **Metric Thresholds**, and **Other Collected Items** tabs of this screen. You can add or delete monitoring template metrics in the **Metrics Threshold** tab.

You can select a monitoring template from the list and click on the **Apply** button. This option allows you to apply the template to one or more targets of the same type. When you click on the **Apply** button, you can select targets to which this template needs to be applied.

When the template is applied to a target, metrics settings and corrective actions are copied to the target. The metrics collection schedule is also copied over to the target. This copy is governed by the following two apply options:

- **Template will completely replace all metric settings in the target**: Any existing metric settings will be replaced by the template's settings

- **Template will only override metrics that are common to both template and target**: Only common metrics are updated with the settings specified on the template

When the template is changed, it also needs to be reapplied.

We walked through the various aspects of managing events and alerts. Fine tuning the events and corrective actions are one of the most dynamic aspects of managing a cloud environment. Great care should be taken in making sure that the resiliency of the cloud is enhanced by correct usage of the powerful mechanism of events and notifications.

Notifications

Before we talk in detail about incident management, let's briefly talk about notifications. When an event generates an alert, a notification is dispatched to the administrators and people whose attention is required. Oracle Enterprise Manager can send e-mail, SNMP traps, and pager notifications. Additionally, custom scripts can be triggered as part of the notification process. There are two major configurations to set up correct notifications:

- **Notification methods**: Based on the type of notifications you need to send, you will need to set up the delivery medium. For example, you need to set up an SMTP server to send e-mail notifications.

- **Rules**: Instruct Enterprise Manager to take some specific action when the event is triggered

Incident management

In this section, we will take a detailed look at the incident management capabilities of Oracle Enterprise Manager.

We briefly talked about events. They form the basis of an incident management system. An event is something significant happening out of the normal operating circumstances. While events suggest some sort of failure, a successful completion of a background job can also trigger an event. Hence, our definition of events needs to include both the exception conditions and compliance issues. Events are coupled with a consistent set of management features and corrective actions.

Common types of events supported by Oracle Enterprise Manager:

- **Target availability**: This event can be used to track if the target is up or down or its agent is unreachable.

- **Metric alert**: This event is generated when an alert occurs for a metric on the target. For example, CPU utilization exceeding a certain percentage.

- **Job status change**: Any change to a standard enterprise manager job is an event.

- **Compliance standard rule violation**: This event is raised when a configured compliance standard metric is breached.

- **High availability**: This event is generally associated with database states, such as database shutdown or startup.

- **Service level agreement alert**: This event is triggered when a service level is violated. As we discussed earlier, in an enterprise cloud environment, it is imperative to make sure that the SLAs are strongly adhered to. For both internal as well as external customers, correct responses to SLA violations must be of the highest priority.

For each of these event types, their severity denotes how critical the event is. The following severity levels are supported:

- **Fatal**: This severity level indicates that the underlying service is not available. For example, a database is down. This is the highest level of severity and can only be associated with the target availability event type.

- **Critical**: The underlying service or host is either not functional or is nearing a failure state. Usually immediate attention is required for such events.

- **Warning**: The underlying service or host is functional but attention should be given to the condition of the service or the host.

- **Advisory**: Care should be taken regarding the current state of the service although there is no need for an immediate attention.

- **Informational**: To indicate certain conditions that do not require any attention but are displayed for information. This type of event cannot be used to create incidents nor do they appear in the incident management workflow.

Incidents

Events will draw your attention to an anomaly but it is often unpractical to work on each of these events individually. Usually events of the same type are grouped together and fixed altogether. For example, if 10 databases raised events related to storage space, all these events can be resolved by adding more storage to the database master node. Such events are grouped and handled as incidents. Incidents usually indicate a larger service disruption or reduced quality of service. Failure of configuration on systems not impacting the service can also be considered an incident; for example, failure of one of the disks from a mirrored set. Incidents can be a single event or a group of events. Incidents are tracked, assigned to technical staff, monitored, and resolved.

Oracle Enterprise Manager defines a workflow-like structure to track the lifecycle of an incident. When an incident is created, Oracle Enterprise Manager initiates a workflow that allows you to track the state of an incident through various phases of that workflow.

Incidents can be created automatically by using rules or rulesets or you can create incidents manually by selecting events and assign incidents to them.

When an incident is created, by default it is put into **New** state. When the incident is assigned to someone for further action, it goes into **Work in Progress** state. Once the issue is identified or fixed, it can be put into **Closed** state. Once the fixed issue is verified as fixed, it can be put into **Resolved** state.

Apart from the state associated to the incident, you can configure what should happen when the priority of the incident changes. For example, when an issue goes from medium priority to high priority, we can send an alert to higher management or a different system administration team. There can be several levels of support, such as L1, L2, and L3, and they can respond to different priorities of alerts.

Apart from the priority of the incidents, you can assign escalation levels (none, level 1 to 5). These escalation levels trigger notifications to a higher level of administration to make sure the incident gets correct visibility and action.

As incidents can be composed of several events, incidents inherit the highest severity from all the events.

Rules and rulesets

You can automate related actions to an event or an incident by setting up rules and rulesets. Incidents can be created, notifications sent, and various workflow steps can be automatically triggered via rules and rulesets.

A rule is an instruction to Oracle Enterprise Manager to take specific steps when an incident or an event occurs. These rules can range from simply sending notifications to appropriate people to taking complex steps, such as creating incidents or editing incidents. Typically, useful rules are conditional. For example, if the severity of an event is warning, send a notification to L3 support team, but if the severity becomes high, send the notification to system administration and also send a pager alert to the higher management team.

These rules can be combined into rulesets. Rulesets can be applied to a group or type of targets. Rules within a ruleset are evaluated in the order they are defined.

For example, a typical ruleset might look like the following:

- **Rule name**: Ruleset for stage instance
- **Applies to**: Stage
- **Type**: Enterprise
    - ° **Rule 1**: Target down
        - **Criteria**: Database instance down
        - **Action**: Create incident and set priority as high
    - ° **Rule 2**: E-mail notification
        - **Criteria**: All incidents with fatal or critical severity
        - **Action 1**: If severity = fatal, send pager to L3 admin and send e-mail
        - **Action 2**: If severity = critical, send e-mail to L3 admin

As we can see here, the rules are executed in the order they are defined in the ruleset. There are two types of rulesets:

- **Enterprise rulesets**: This is a restricted type because it can perform all the supported actions. An administrator must have the privilege "create enterprise ruleset" granted on the enterprise ruleset object to be able to create or modify these types of rules.

- **Private rulesets**: Sometimes an administrator wants to set up a notification hierarchy separate from the enterprise one. In that case, he can create a private ruleset to route notifications to a different path than the one defined as per the enterprise ruleset. This type of ruleset can only be used to send notifications.

Oracle Enterprise Manager packs a set of default rulesets for incident creation based on the standard scenarios. These rulesets are constant and cannot be modified. You can always copy these rules and modify the copied rules according to your needs.

As we saw earlier, rules are the backbone of incident management. Rulesets are composed of one or more cascading rules. We will take a detailed look at the rules and how they are configured.

Rules intercept incoming conditions and decide the reactive action for those. Rules are composed of two parts:

- **Criteria**: Event or incident for which the rule is applicable
- **Actions**: One or more operations on the criteria which will decide the outcome of the rule

Let's take an example to understand this further.

Rule	Order	Criteria	Condition	Action
CPU-space threshold	1st	CPU percent and database storage space event of warning or critical severity		Create an incident
Notify e-mail – pager	2nd	Warning or critical severity	If severity = warning	Send e-mail notification to L3 support
			If severity = critical	Send pager alert to DBA team
Escalation	3rd	Incidents are not set to in-progress state for more than 2 hours		Escalate the issue by setting escalation level to 1

As you can see, the first rule applies to multiple metrics events. Rule 2 is applied based on the severity of the event and rule 3 is applied based on the time factor. Each rule within the ruleset is applied to an event or an incident. Rule application criteria can be selected as:

- Apply the rule to incoming events or updated events only
- Apply the rule to critical events only

Rules are applied based on the following logic:

- If one of the rules in the ruleset results in creating an incident, Oracle Enterprise Manager completes matching the event to any additional rule. Oracle Enterprise Manager then matches the created incident against all rulesets to see if any rule matches with the new incident.
- If an incoming event is associated with an incident, Oracle Enterprise Manager applies all rules to that event.
- If during application of the rule the state of the incident is changed, Oracle Enterprise Manager aborts the application and re-applies the rules to the incident.

For each type of rule, we can define actions. Examples of these actions are: create an incident based on the type of an event or send an e-mail notification to a certain group of people.

Following actions are allowed on the rule application:

- Email notification
- Page notification
- Advanced notification
- Send SNMP trap
- Run operations system command
- Run PL/SQL procedure
- Create an incident
- Set workflow attributes
- Create a helpdesk ticket

With this information in hand, let's see how we can create these components to set up a useful monitoring infrastructure. Oracle Enterprise Manager provides **Incident Manager** dashboard as a single place to manage the monitoring infrastructure. You can navigate to **Enterprise | Monitoring | Incident Manager**.

To create rulesets, you can navigate to **Setup | Incidents | Incident Rules**.

You can either edit the existing rules or create new ones in this page. While creating the rulesets, you can choose to apply the ruleset only to a few target types based on the target's lifecycle status value.

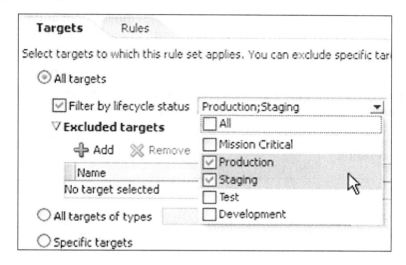

In the previous screenshot, you can see that we are applying the ruleset for targets that have lifecycle status as staging or production. This makes it easier for us to restrict the rule based on criteria other than the target type.

You can create rules that create incidents, as follow:

1. Navigate to the **Setup | Incidents** menu and select **Incident Rules**.

2. In the **Incident Rules** page, you can search for the rule/ruleset. You can search by target name or other parameters to locate the rulesets that manage the targets.

3. If there are no existing rulesets, you can create the ruleset. Rules can be created as part of the ruleset creation.

4. Select the ruleset that will contain the new rule and click on the **Edit** button. Further, in the **Rules** tab of the **Edit Rule Set** page, you need to click on the **Create** button and select **Incoming events and updates to events**. In the **Create New Rule** wizard, you can provide information to create the rule.

5. You can select the event type for the rule, for example, **Metric Alert**.

6. You can specify metric alerts by selecting **Specific Metrics**. Click on the + button to launch the metric selector. On the **Select Specific Metric Alert** page, select the target type.

7. .You can also select the severity and corrective action status.

8. Click on the **Next** button on the wizard step. Click on the **+** button to add the actions to occur when the event is triggered.

9. If you chose to create incident, you can assign the incident automatically to a particular set of user and set the priority of the incident on creation.

10. Similarly, you can create rules to manage escalation of incidents. In the same wizard flow we discussed previously, you can create such rules.

11. In the **Rules** tab of the **Edit Rule Set** page, click on **Create** and select **Newly created incidents or updates to incidents**.

In the wizard, you can provide rule creation details, as shown in the following screenshot:

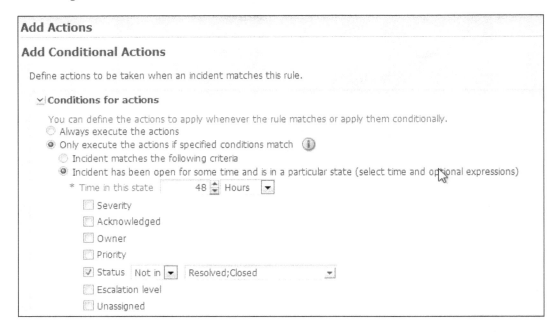

You can set up your rule based on various options listed here. If you want the rule to be applied to all newly created incidents or when the incident is updated with fatal severity, select the **Specific Incidents** option and add the condition **Severity is Fatal**. You can select the **Always execute the actions** or **Only execute the actions if specified conditions match** option to conditionally execute the rule. If you choose the latter, you can define several parameters that determine the rule execution. For example, you can select the **Incident has been open for some time and is in a particular state** option to select a time period and various other parameters like incident states.

In the **Update Incident** screen (shown in the following screenshot), you can specify notification details in this wizard step to set up notification rules. You can also automatically assign the incident to a specific person and set priority, status, and escalation level to specific values.

You can also set escalation parameters for the problem while creating the rule. In the same wizard flow we discussed earlier, navigate to the **Select Type of Rule to Create | Newly created problems or updates to problems** dialog and click on **Continue**.

Select **Specific Problems** and add the criteria that should trigger incident escalation. For example, set **Incident Count** greater than or equal to 10.

There are several variations you can set up at this point to make sure you create rules for appropriate escalation.

Now that we have the necessary rules and rulesets configured, we can take a look at how we can work with incidents using Oracle Enterprise Manager.

As we discussed, **Incident Manager** is the single interface pane where you can manage your incidents and view a very detailed history of incidents.

Oracle Enterprise Manager provides multiple access points that allow you to find out what needs to be worked on. Most of the tasks can be done via **Incident Manager Console**.

To search for incidents, navigate to **Enterprise | Monitoring | Incident Manager**. You can see that the **Incident Manager** page contains a plethora of information regarding the incidents and allows you to configure and manage the view as per your convenience.

In the **Views** region on the left, click on **Search**. You can click on criteria applicable to the search and if you want you can add fields to the search. Click on **Get Results** to view the list of incidents matching your query. The following screenshot shows the default **Incident Manager** view:

The **Incident Manager** page lets you customize the views to your needs. In the **Views** region, you can click on **Search**. Perform a normal incident search as we discussed earlier. Make sure you add all search criteria you want in your custom view. Once the search result is displayed, you can click on arrange the column layout according to your requirements. Once you have finalized the view, you can click on the **Create View** button and save the view. The following screenshot shows a customized view:

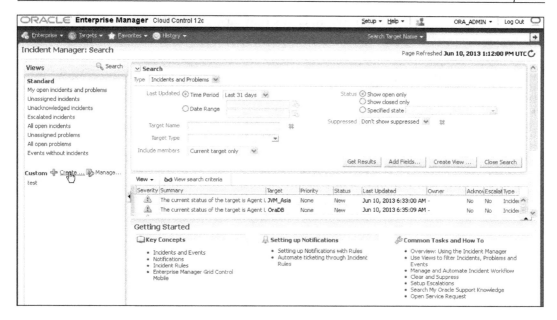

A detailed view of all open incidents will help you quickly sort and filter incidents as per their state, priority, and escalation levels, as shown in the following screenshot:

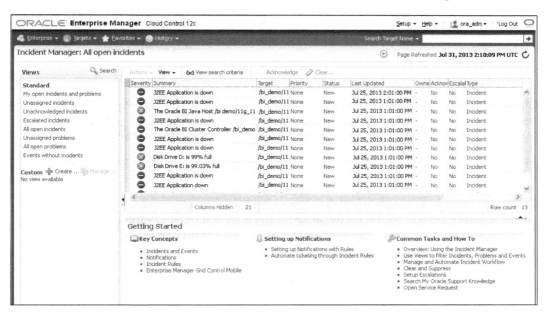

For each target, you can drill down to check that target's incident history in **Incident Manager**, as shown in the following screenshot:

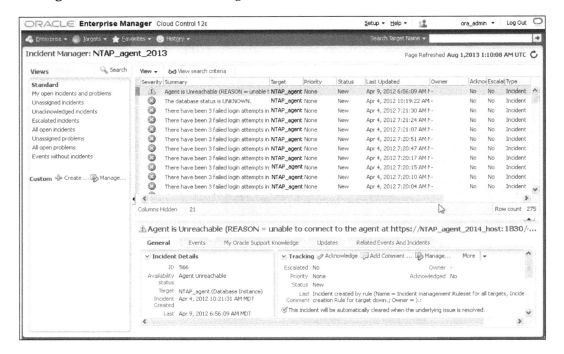

Responding to incidents

You can respond to incidents from **Incident Manager**. As you will learn, **Incident Manager** gets to become your central place of activity if you are responding to several incidents in a day or you are monitoring the incidents on a regular basis. You can go to **Incident Manager** by navigating to **Enterprise | Monitoring**.

To quickly check incidents assigned to you, use the view **My Open Incidents and Problems**.

To start working on the incident, you can select the incident and click on the **Acknowledge** button in the **General** tab. This action moves the incident into work in progress state and prevents repeated notifications. You can also perform the following actions on the incident:

- Add a comment to give an idea on what you are working on
- Edit the summary information
- Create a support ticket
- Clear an incident

Once you resolve the incident, you can clear the incident and add the work order summary if required.

You can respond to multiple incidents in similar fashion. In the view **My Open Incidents and Problems**, you can select multiple incidents in bulk (by pressing the *Ctrl* or *Shift* key while selecting incidents).

Click on the **Action** drop-down menu and you can select the following response actions:

- **Acknowledge**: This indicates that you have checked the incident and you intend to work on it. This action will make you owner of the incident and prevent any repeated notifications.
- **Manage**: You can select several subactions for this:
    - **Acknowledge**: If you manually assign an incident to yourself, it is automatically acknowledged.
    - **Assign to**: You can use this option to assign the incident to a specific person or yourself.
    - **Prioritization**: You can set the priority to **None, Urgent, Very High, High, Medium**, or **Low**.
    - **Incident Status**: Indicates the state of the incident. You can set this field to **Work in Progress, Resolved**, or any custom status.
    - **Escalation Level**: You can set the escalation level through 1 to 5.
    - **Comment**: You can add comments for the action
- **Suppress**: You can suppress the incident to remove it from the notification queue and work on it at a later period in time. This can be useful if you know that another incident or problem is going to resolve this particular incident and you want to remove this incident from incident reports and stop any notifications for it.
- **Clear**: Incidents can be cleared when they are resolved.

The **Incident Manager** page allows you to create an incident manually. You can search for an event from the main page and click on the **Create Incident** button from the action menu when you select the event.

Summary

As the complexity of cloud infrastructure increases, challenges of scalability and maintenance increase significantly. For any organization, it becomes very important to respond and resolve issues immediately and minimize impact on internal or external customers. As we discussed in this chapter, Oracle Enterprise Manager offers an exhaustive set of monitoring mechanisms. We also saw how we can set up some of these features, such as rules, rulesets, and notifications.

We also discussed how we can set up effective notification rules to make sure support and administration teams are is always aware of any incidents. The next chapter focuses on using the Oracle Enterprise Manager programmable interface using Cloud APIs and EMCLIs.

5
Cloud APIs

By definition, cloud computing is meant to be flexible and elastic. Most of its power comes from the fact that most of the components that constitute the infrastructure are loosely coupled. Devices can be plugged in, removed, reconfigured, and realigned without any effect on the overall cloud infrastructure.

Most cloud management systems recognize this fact and try to offer management tools that give the most flexibility to the end-user. However, there will always be cases when you will require a more fine-grained programmatic control over your cloud infrastructure. It is difficult to imagine the current state of cloud computing without the maturity of the underlying programmatic interfaces provided by the cloud providers.

All large cloud providers like Amazon AWS provide an extensive set of programming interfaces in the form of APIs or web services to configure and utilize the infrastructure and build custom interfaces.

As we are moving towards a completely connected world, most of the cloud services have started providing web service interfaces as opposed to the traditional API model where you required an authenticated SSH session to perform any programmatic operations.

Oracle Enterprise Manager provides command-line interface (CLI) and RESTful (Representational State Transfer) APIs that use HTTP verbs as the transport mechanism and handle the communication using widely standardized JSON (JavaScript Object Notation) format. In this chapter, we will take a look at the various Enterprise Manager Cloud APIs and how to use them.

Topics covered in this chapter are:

- Using Enterprise Manager Cloud APIs and CLIs
- Enterprise Manager IaaS APIs
- Enterprise Manager DBaaS APIs
- Chargeback EMCLIs

Using Enterprise Manager Cloud APIs and CLIs

Oracle Enterprise Manager installs necessary components to support RESTful Cloud APIs and there is no extra setup required to support them. Oracle Enterprise Manager contains Java client APIs as a package. To start using Java Client APIs, you need to make sure you have **Java Development Kit (JDK)** and **Java Runtime Environment (JRE) 1.6** or later installed. You can check the installation by issuing the following commands:

```
bash-3.2$ java -version
java version "1.7.0_25"
Java(TM) SE Runtime Environment (build 1.7.0_25-b15)
Java HotSpot(TM) 64-Bit Server VM (build 23.25-b01, mixed mode)
bash-3.2$ javac -version
javac 1.7.0_25
```

To install the Java client API package, enter the following command as the root:

```
bash-3.2$ cd /home/oracle_em/src/dvd/Linux_i686/Product/components/
packages/
bash-3.2$ rpm -i orcl-sysman-iaas-api.rpm
```

Replace /home/oracle_em in the above command with the actual path on your Linux machine. The APIs will be installed under /opt/oracle/iaas/iaas-java-api.

Additionally, you will need to install a package called Cloud Infrastructure CLI. This package is also part of Oracle Enterprise Manager installation. You can install this package by running the following command as root:

```
bash-3.2$ cd <repo>/src/dvd/Linux_i686/Product/components/packages/
bash-3.2$ rpm -i orcl-sysman-iaas-cli.rpm
```

Before you can use these CLIs, you will need to make sure they are available in the environment variable. You can set the `IAAS_HOME` environment variable to include the directory containing these APIs. Either you can add the `IAAS_HOME` environment variable in the initialization scripts (`.bashrc` or `.profile`) or manually set it on the command prompt as follows:

```
export IAAS_HOME=/opt/oracle/iaas/cli
```

The cloud administrator will need to first create an access key to use cloud APIs to manage resources. These access keys need to be passed to each of the API calls to authenticate the call.

Also, if you intend to manage resources via the cloud APIs, you will need to first create the vDC account. Also to use **Enterprise Manager Command Line Interface (EMCLI)**, you will need to download and install the necessary `.jar` file from the Enterprise Manager Installation.

Enterprise Manager IaaS APIs

RESTful APIs operate on resources and these resources are part of the URI scheme for the Cloud API REST calls. IaaS consists of the computing, network, storage, and other virtualized resources and it is important to understand how they are all related. The following diagram gives an overview of how the IaaS resources are interconnected. Each of these resources can be accessed and modified via the corresponding RESTful cloud APIs.

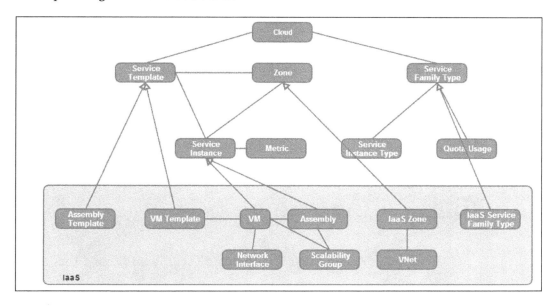

While we can not cover all the resources and the operations supported on them, let's take an indicative example of how a particular operation via a RESTful cloud API will look like. IaaS APIs provide the following operations to be performed.

- Create, delete, list, search, and update a service instance
- Add a VM disk

Let's say that we want to create a VM programmatically using RESTful Cloud APIs. A VM is a service instance of the type `iaas` that we will be creating via the REST API. We will send a POST request to the `iaas` zone where the VM will reside. You can send these requests programmatically or via any custom self-service tool that supports the REST calls.

The request-response dialog of this POST call will look like:

```
Request:

Method : POST https://<host>:<port>/em/cloud/iaas/servicetemplate/vm/
oracle%3AdefaultService%3Aem%3Aprovisioning%3A1%3Acmp%3AVirtualization
%3ATemplate%<session_identifier>%3A0.1
Content-type: application/oracle.com.cloud.common.VM+json
Body: {
  "based_on":"/em/cloud/iaas/servicetemplate/vm/oracle%3AdefaultServ
ice%3Aem%3Aprovisioning%3A1%3Acmp%3AVirtualization%3ATemplate%<sesi
on_identifier>%3A0.1",
  "cpu" : [2,0],
  "memory" : "1024",
  "params":{
    "server_prefix":"TESTZONE",
    "vnc_password":"vnc_pass",
    "root_password":"root_pass"
  }
}
Response:
{
  "uri" : "/em/cloud/iaas/server/byrequest/11" ,
  "name" : "TEST VM Creation 21231123111121" ,
  "resource_state" :      {
      "state" : "INITIATED" ,
      "messages" :
      [
        {
            "text" : "The Request with ID '11' is scheduled with Job
```

```
Id 'C655621332DH2378432DSAA3432431343133'" ,
          "date" : "2013-09-10T13:09:02+0000"
        }
    ]
  } ,
"context_id" : "11" ,
"media_type" : "application/oracle.com.cloud.common.VM+json" ,
"service_family_type" : "iaas" ,
"created" : "2013-09-10T13:09:02+0000"
}
```

An important thing to notice is the way the URL is formed. Notice that iaas and servicetemplate are part of the URL verbs and that conveys the intent of the POST call to Oracle Enterprise Manager. The response that this call receives shows which job was triggered for this task. Similarly, Enterprise Manager Command Line Interface (EMCLI) can be used to execute smaller tasks from the command line or small shell scripts. This is a very useful approach if you do not want to go with the RESTful APIs.

For example, the following set of EMCLI steps will provision an Oracle Database.

1. Retrieve GUID of the deployment procedure:

   ```
   ./emcli get_procedures | grep DB
   …<a few values for GUID>
   C354655454E1010F4453EEE1034579DC, DB_PROV_UPGRADE,
   DbProvUpgradeDP, Upgrade Oracle Database, 1.0, ORACLE
   C354655454E1010F4453EEE1034579DC, DBPROV, SIHA_SIDB_PROC,
   Provision Oracle Database, 1.0, ORACLE
   ```

   Note the GUID against the process SIHA_SIDB_PROC, in our case it's C354655454E1010F4453EEE1034579DC.

2. Create a property file:

   ```
   ./emcli describe_procedure_input -procedure=
   C354655454E1010F4453EEE1034579DC > provdb.properties
   ```

3. Using the property file, submit the provisioning procedure:

   ```
   ./emcli submit_procedure -input_file=data:prov.properties
   -instance="provdb" -procedure= C354655454E1010F4453EEE1034579DC
   Verifying parameters ...
   Schedule not specified, defaults to immediate
   ```

```
C992344243EADAA6788467EE343564F1
Deployment procedure submitted successfully
```

Notice that EMCLIs operate on each action in a sequence. They are useful for non-complex tasks but their usage can get complex when you want to develop applications that handle actions asynchronously.

Enterprise Manager DBaaS APIs

For DBaaS APIs, the following resource models are supported:

- DB Zone (URI Format: `/em/cloud/dbaas/zone/<zone id>`)
- DB Platform Template (URI Format: `/em/cloud/dbaas/dbplatformtemplate/<template id>`)
- DB Platform Instance (URI Format: `/em/cloud/dbaas/dbplatforminstance/byrequest/<request id>`)

These resources act as HTTP verbs for the RESTful APIs. All the resource models support JSON payloads and defined by media type `application/oracle.com.cloud.common.DbPlatformInstance+json`. The following diagram depicts this relationship in more detail:

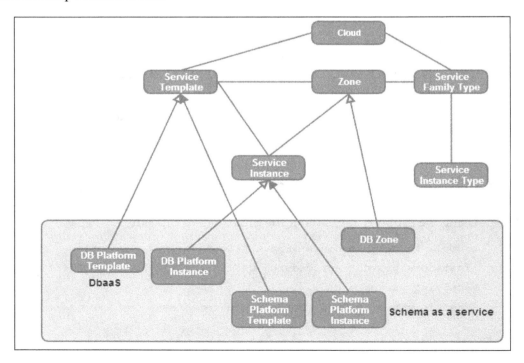

For an example, let's see the request-response dialog for the RESTful API call to describe the type of services that are provided by a service family type:

```
Request:
URI - https://<host:port>/em/cloud/instance_type/
dbPlatformInstance%40dbaas
Method - GET
Response:
{
  "uri" : "/em/cloud/instance_type/dbPlatformInstance%40dbaas" ,
  "name" : "dbPlatformInstance" ,
  "description" : "Db Instance" ,
  "media_type" : "application/oracle.com.cloud.common.
InstanceType+json" ,
  "instance_media_type" : "application/oracle.com.cloud.common.
DbPlatformInstance+json" , ,
  "canonicalLink": "/em/websvcs/restful/extws/cloudservices/service/
v0/ssa/em/cloud/instance_type/dbPlatformInstance%40dbaas"
}
```

As you can see, all the DBaaS resources expose APIs for most common operations. You can also find the equivalent EMCLIs for these actions. The scope of this book will not allow us to take a look at these APIs in detail but this discussion will equip you to understand their basic behavior.

Chargeback EMCLIs

Chargeback verbs for EMCLIs can be used to quickly track chargebacks. You can use custom charge items to create separate chargeback rules from the ones defined by Enterprise Manager. We will go through some examples to illustrate the usage of chargeback EMCLIs.

- Example: List the items registered to chargeback

    ○ EMCLI verb: `list_charge_item_candidates`

    ○ Usage:

    ```
    emcli list_charge_item_candidates -target_type="oracle_
    database" -source_data_type="metric"
    ```

    Value of `target_type` can be `oracle_database`, `oracle_vm_guest`, `host`, `oracle_pdb`, or `weblogic_j2eeserver`.

- Example: Create a charge item
    - ○ EMCLI verb: `create_charge_item`
    - ○ Usage:

```
emcli create_charge_item -input_file="property_file:/home/
vantani/db.prop"
```

You need to provide a property file that contains all the necessary values for the creation of the charge item. Property file for this verb contains values in format <key>=<value>.

- Example: Delete a charge item
    - ○ EMCLI verb: `delete_charge_item`
    - ○ Usage:

```
emcli delete_charge_item -target_type="oracle_database"
-item_name="sample_db"
```

- Example: Retrieve metering data
    - ○ EMCLI Verb: `get_metering_data`
    - ○ Usage:

```
emcli get_metering_data -start_date=08152013 -end_date=-
09152013 -target_type=oracle_database
```

The preceding command gives collected metering for all the Oracle database targets registered with Enterprise Manager Chargeback.

Summary

While Oracle Enterprise Manager gives you elaborate options to configure and monitor targets via the Enterprise Manager UI, there may be times when you need more programmatic control over your cloud infrastructure. Oracle Enterprise Manager RESTful Cloud APIs and EMCLIs serve this purpose quite well.

Most of the advanced use cases can be covered by using these APIs effectively and building your own solutions.

Index

H

high availability event 72
host option 45

I

IaaS (Infrastructure as a Service)
  about 7, 31
  Infrastructure Cloud Home page 31, 32
  OVM Manager home page 32, 33
  virtualization targets, managing 34
  virtualization targets, viewing 34
  Virtual Server Pool home page 34, 36
  virtual servers, editing 36, 37
  virtual servers, maintaining 37
IaaS APIs 87-89
IaaS model 15
IaaS self-service portal
  machine sizes, setting up 38
  provisioning request settings,
       modifying 38, 39
  roles, modifying 39, 40
  setting up 37
  software components, modifying 40
incident management 72
Incident Manager page 80
incidents
  about 73
  responding to 82, 83
Infrastructure as a Service model. *See* IaaS
       model
Infrastructure Cloud
  home page 31, 32
installer method
  using 49
Intelligent Platform Management
       Interface (IPMI) 37

J

Java Development Kit (JDK) 86
Java Runtime Environment (JRE) 1.6 86
job status change event 72

L

logical unit number (LUN) 52

M

MAC addresses
  generating 21
metric alert event 72
moving window baseline 69

N

Network Attached Storage (NAS) 25
Network file system (NFS) 25
networking
  about 21
  creating 22-24
  MAC addresses, generating 21
  network profile, creating 24, 25
  VLAN groups, creating 22
notifications
  about 71
  methods 71
  rules 71

O

OMS Agent Filesystem Location 8
OMS Shared Filesystem Location 9
Oracle Enterprise Manager Cloud
       Control 12c 7
Oracle Virtual Machine Manager
  home page 32, 33
Oracle VM Manager
  about 16
  adding, as Enterprise Manager target 16, 17
  certificates, importing in agent keystore 16
  discovering 18-20
  local storage 25
  Network Attached Storage (NAS) 25
  Storage Attached Network (SAN) 25
  Virtual Server 20
OVM Zone option 46

Thank you for buying
Managing IaaS and DBaaS Clouds with Oracle
Enterprise Manager Cloud Control 12*c*

About Packt Publishing

Packt, pronounced 'packed', published its first book "Mastering phpMyAdmin for Effective MySQL Management" in April 2004 and subsequently continued to specialize in publishing highly focused books on specific technologies and solutions.

Our books and publications share the experiences of your fellow IT professionals in adapting and customizing today's systems, applications, and frameworks. Our solution based books give you the knowledge and power to customize the software and technologies you're using to get the job done. Packt books are more specific and less general than the IT books you have seen in the past. Our unique business model allows us to bring you more focused information, giving you more of what you need to know, and less of what you don't.

Packt is a modern, yet unique publishing company, which focuses on producing quality, cutting-edge books for communities of developers, administrators, and newbies alike. For more information, please visit our website: www.packtpub.com.

About Packt Enterprise

In 2010, Packt launched two new brands, Packt Enterprise and Packt Open Source, in order to continue its focus on specialization. This book is part of the Packt Enterprise brand, home to books published on enterprise software – software created by major vendors, including (but not limited to) IBM, Microsoft and Oracle, often for use in other corporations. Its titles will offer information relevant to a range of users of this software, including administrators, developers, architects, and end users.

Writing for Packt

We welcome all inquiries from people who are interested in authoring. Book proposals should be sent to author@packtpub.com. If your book idea is still at an early stage and you would like to discuss it first before writing a formal book proposal, contact us; one of our commissioning editors will get in touch with you.

We're not just looking for published authors; if you have strong technical skills but no writing experience, our experienced editors can help you develop a writing career, or simply get some additional reward for your expertise.

Apache CloudStack Cloud Computing

ISBN: 9-781-78216-010-6   Paperback: 294 pages

Leverage the power of CloudStack and learn to extend the CloudStack environment

1. Install, deploy, and manage a cloud service using CloudStack

2. Step-by-step instructions on setting up and running the leading open source cloud platform CloudStack

3. Set up an IaaS cloud environment using CloudStack

Getting Started with Oracle Public Cloud

ISBN: 9-781-78217-810-1   Paperback: 96 pages

Master the core concepts of Oracle Public Cloud and its services - Java, Database, Transition, Storage, and Messaging

1. Get to grips with the core concepts of Cloud computing and Oracle Public Cloud services

2. Learn the best practices to be followed while using Oracle Public Cloud

3. This book will reveal the power of Oracle Public Cloud and show you how you can use this power to your advantage

Please check **www.PacktPub.com** for information on our titles

OpenNebula 3 Cloud Computing

ISBN: 9-781-84951-746-1   Paperback: 314 pages

Set up, manage, and maintain your Cloud and learn solutions for datacenter virtualization with this step-by-step practical guide

1. Take advantage of open source distributed file-systems for storage scalability and high-availability

2. Build-up, manage and maintain your Cloud without previous knowledge of virtualization and cloud computing

3. Install and configure every supported hypervisor: KVM, Xen, VMware

Getting Started with Citrix® CloudPortal™

ISBN: 9-781-78217-682-4   Paperback: 128 pages

Get acquainted with Citrix Systems™ CPSM and CPBM in order to administer cloud services smoothly and comprehensively

1. Overview of CPSM and CPBM architectures, and planning CPSM and CPBM

2. Become efficient in product management, workflow management, and billing and pricing management

3. Provision services efficiently to cloud consumers and clients

Please check **www.PacktPub.com** for information on our titles